EGYPT IN 1800

EGYPT IN 1800

SCENES FROM NAPOLEON'S
DESCRIPTION DE L'EGYPTE

Edited by Robert Anderson
and Ibrahim Fawzy

BARRIE & JENKINS
LONDON

First published in Great Britain in 1988 by
Barrie & Jenkins Ltd
289 Westbourne Grove, London W11 2QA

British Library Cataloguing in Publication Data

[Description de L'Egypte. *Selections*] Egypt in
  1800: Scenes from Napoleon's Description
  de l'Egypte.
  1. Egypt ——— Description and travel
  I. Anderson, Robert   II. Fawzy, Ibrahim
  916.2'043   DT53

  ISBN 0-7126-2006-0

Designed by David Hopper and produced by IMPADS Associates, London
Printed in Great Britain by BAS Printers, Over Wallop, Hampshire

CONTENTS

The savants who accompanied Napoleon's expeditionary force to Egypt in 1798 recorded their impressions of the country under three main heads. They described ancient Egypt, modern Egypt, and the natural history of Egypt. There was in addition a volume of maps. For the monumental *Description de l'Egypte* 900 plates were produced, and by the time the second edition was complete more than 30 years after Napoleon landed in Egypt, there were 26 volumes of text and 11 elephant folio volumes of plates.

This selective reproduction of plates from the *Description* covers the Napoleonic ancient and modern Egypt, of which the original 600 plates have been reduced to slightly less than a third of their number. The ancient Egypt of the turn of the 18th century was different from what we know now. Temples were filled with debris, but newly discovered tombs were in wonderful condition. Shrines that have since disappeared were described and delineated by the savants. The modern Egypt dealt with in the *Description* is the Egypt of the Turkish Empire just before Mohamed Ali's decisive leadership brought her into touch with the latest in European thought. Much was traditional, much was characteristic of Islam at its finest. Cairo was a world city of legendary beauty and riches, and the artists of the *Description* revelled in the opportunity to perpetuate its architectural splendour as well as the appearance and occupations of its inhabitants.

Robert Anderson
Ibrahim Fawzy

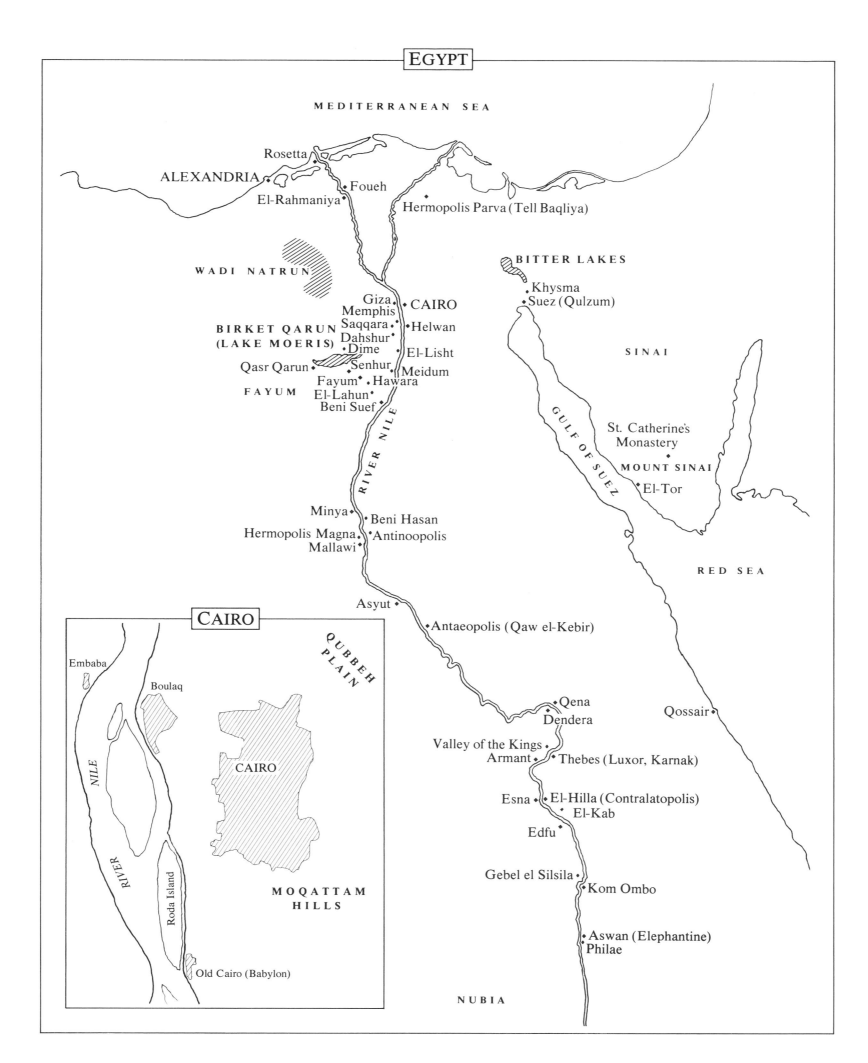

EGYPT

MEDITERRANEAN SEA

Rosetta

ALEXANDRIA

Foueh

El-Rahmaniya

Hermopolis Parva (Tell Baqliya)

WADI NATRUN

BITTER LAKES

Khysma

Suez (Qulzum)

Giza
Memphis
Saqqara
Dahshur
Dime

CAIRO

Helwan

BIRKET QARUN
(LAKE MOERIS)

El-Lisht

SINAI

Qasr Qarun
Senhur
Fayum
Hawara
El-Lahun
Beni Suef

Meidum

FAYUM

RIVER NILE

GULF OF SUEZ

St. Catherine's
Monastery

MOUNT SINAI

El-Tor

Minya
Beni Hasan
Hermopolis Magna
Antinoopolis
Mallawi

RED SEA

Asyut

Antaeopolis (Qaw el-Kebir)

CAIRO

Embaba

Boulaq

QUBBEH
PLAIN

NILE

CAIRO

RIVER

Roda Island

MOQATTAM
HILLS

Old Cairo (Babylon)

Qena
Dendera

Qossair

Valley of the Kings
Armant
Thebes (Luxor, Karnak)

Esna
El-Hilla (Contralatopolis)
El-Kab

Edfu

Gebel el Silsila
Kom Ombo

Aswan (Elephantine)
Philae

NUBIA

TIME CHART

B.C.*

3100-2890 1st dynasty; Menes first king of the Two Lands; Memphis founded.

2613-2494 4th dynasty; period of the greatest Old Kingdom pyramid builders, Sneferu, Khufu (Cheops), Khafre (Chephren), and Menkaure (Mycerinus).

2130-2040 10th dynasty; part of the First Intermediate Period.

1991-1786 12th dynasty; zenith of Middle Kingdom power, with new capital at Lisht; Sesostris I (1971-1928), Sesostris II (1897-1878), Sesostris III (1878-1843), Amenemhat III (1842-1797).

1660-1552 15th dynasty; kings of Asiatic origin, ruling Egypt from their Delta capital, Avaris; known as the Hyksos, part of the Second Intermediate Period.

1552-1295 18th dynasty; New Kingdom extension of the Egyptian empire, culminating in the prosperous reign of Amenophis III (1390-1352); political collapse of the Amarna period; Amenophis I (1527-1506), Tuthmosis I (1506-1493), Hatshepsut (1479-1458), Tuthmosis III (1479-1425), Tuthmosis IV (1401-1390), Amenophis III (1390-1352), Tutankhamun (1336-1327), Horemheb (1323-1295).

1295-1188 19th dynasty; period of massive buildings but much exterior conflict, notably with the Hittites; Sethos I (1294-1279), Ramesses II (1279-1212), Merneptah (1212-1202), Sethos II (1202-1196).

1188-1069 20th dynasty; battles against the Sea Peoples; evidence of internal disorder in disturbance of Royal Mummies; Ramesses III (1186-1154), Ramesses IV (1154-1148).

1069-945 21st dynasty; two separate capitals; at Tanis in the Delta, line of rulers including Siamun; at Thebes, power with the High Priests including Pinodjem.

945-715 22nd dynasty; rulers from Libya with capital at Bubastis in the Delta.

747-656 25th dynasty; Nubian rulers from Kush; Taharqa (690-664) the great builder among them.

664-525 26th dynasty; capital at Sais in the Delta; Psammetichus I (664-610).

380-343 30th dynasty; the last native rulers of ancient Egypt; Nectanebo I (380-362), Nectanebo II (360-343).

332-305 Macedonian kings; conquest of Alexander the Great (332-323); foundation of Alexandria, 332; Philip Arrhidaeus (323-317).

305-30 The Ptolemies; Ptolemy I (305-282) a general of Alexander the Great; Ptolemy II Philadelphus (284-246) had the Pharos constructed; Ptolemy III (246-222) started temple at Edfu; Ptolemy V (205-180) is honoured in the Rosetta Stone; Ptolemy VI (180-145) started temples of Kom Ombo and Esna; Ptolemy IX (116-107) mentioned in the crypts of the Dendera temple; Ptolemy XII (80-51), father of Cleopatra the Great and twice restored to his throne by Roman arms; Cleopatra the Great (51-30), antagonist of Rome; Caesarion, her son supposedly by Julius Caesar.

30 B.C.-A.D.395 Egypt a Roman province, with imperial governors; Augustus (27 B.C.-A.D. 14), Tiberius (14-37), Caligula (37-41), Claudius (41-54), Nero (54-68), Domitian (81-96), Trajan (98-117), Hadrian (117-138), Antoninus

A.D.

Pius (138-161), Marcus Aurelius (161-180), Lucius Verus (161-169), Alexander Severus (222-235), Decius (249-251), Diocletian (285-305); first beginnings of Christianity in Egypt; St. Antony established a cell in the desert near Beni Suef in 285; start of monastic movement.

395-640 Egypt a Byzantine province; Council of Chalcedon in 451; rupture between the Coptic Orthodox and other Christian churches; Justinian (527-565) closes temples of Philae.

641 Conquest of Egypt by Amr Ibn el-As for the Rashidun caliphs; foundation of Fustat (later known as Misr), capital of Egypt.

766-809 Harun el-Rashid, Abbasid caliph of Baghdad.

868 Ibn Tulun governor of Egypt for the Abbasid caliphs; mosque of Ibn Tulun built (876-879).

969-1171 Egypt ruled by 11 Fatimid caliphs.

969 Foundation of El-Qahira (Cairo), capital of Egypt.

996-1021 El-Hakim ruler of Egypt; his mosque built 990-1013.

1087 Northern extension of the Cairo city walls by Badr el-Gamali.

1168 Egypt attacked by the Second Crusade; Fustat burned to avert its capture.

1171-1199 Salah el-Din (Saladin) ruler of Egypt; fortification of the citadel at Cairo and southern extension of city walls.

1249 Damietta captured by the Sixth Crusade. St. Louis taken captive by the Egyptians in Mansura.

1250-1382 Egypt ruled by 24 Bahri Mameluke sultans; their troops quartered on Roda Island.

1294-1340 Sultan El-Nasir Mohamed in power; constructed the aqueduct, and a mosque on the citadel.

1354-61 Sultan Hasan; his mosque built 1356-62.

1382-1517 Egypt ruled by 23 Burgi Mameluke sultans; their troops quartered on the citadel in Cairo.

1468-98 Sultan Qaitbey; constructed fort on Pharos Island at Alexandria.

1501-16 Sultan Qansuh el-Ghuri; extended Cairo aqueduct and built intake tower.

1517-1805 Egypt a province of the Ottoman Empire, ruled by pashas (viceroys) for the Ottoman sultans; 1571, Sinan Pasha built mosque at Boulaq; 1798-1801, French occupation of Egypt; 2 July 1798, capture of Alexandria; 21 July 1798, battle of the Pyramids; 1 August 1798, battle of the Nile and French fleet destroyed by Nelson; 2 February 1799, occupation of Aswan; 24 August 1799, Napoleon left Egypt; 14 September 1801, French army left Egypt.

1805-48 Mohamed Ali; constructed mosque on the citadel; Mahmudiyya Canal to Alexandria.

1863-92 Khedive Ismail; constructed sweet water canal to Ismailia; Suez Canal opened 1869.

1917-36 King Fuad; built palace at Ras el-Tin, former Pharos Island.

* Most B.C. dates are approximate

4

Robert Anderson, M.A., D.Mus, F.S.A. (Joint Editor). Honorary Secretary of The Egypt Exploration Society from 1971 to 1982, he has worked on the Society's excavations at Saqqara and at Qasr Ibrim in Nubia where he was Administrative Director. He taught hieroglyphs for the Extra-Mural Department of London University for ten years. He has accompanied many Nile cruises as guest lecturer, and appeared in BBC television documentaries on Champollion and Qasr Ibrim. He has contributed to the *Journal of Egyptian Archaeology*, and in 1976 produced the third volume, on musical instruments, for the Catalogue of Egyptian Antiquities in the British Museum. Plates 1-17, 28, 31, 34, 36-56, 58, 59, 67-74.

Ibrahim Fawzy, B.Sc., Ph.D. (Joint Editor). Professor at the Faculty of Engineering, Cairo University. He was Cultural Counsellor for the Egyptian Embassy in London from 1979 to 1983. He founded a quarterly magazine, *The Egyptian Bulletin*, of which he was editor until 1983, and organised the publication of a book called *Ancient Centres of Egyptian Civilization* while in London. From 1975 to 1976 he was a visiting research fellow at University College London, where he had obtained his Ph.D. in 1969.

T.G.H. James, C.B.E., M.A., F.B.A. Keeper of Egyptian Antiquities at the British Museum since 1974, he studied Classics and Egyptology at Oxford University and entered the British Museum in 1951. He has taken part in excavations and epigraphic work in Egypt and published a number of scholarly and general books on Egyptological subjects, including studies of inscriptions and texts on papyri. His most recent publications are *Pharaoh's People* and *Egyptian Painting*. He is also at present Chairman of The Egypt Exploration Society. Plates 18-27, 29, 30, 32, 33, 35.

Geoffrey T. Martin, M.A., Ph. D., F.S.A. Reader in Egyptian Archaeology at University College London from 1980, he became a lecturer there in 1970. He is a Corresponding Member of the German Archaeological Institute in Berlin. He has excavated in Egypt since 1964, and in 1975 was appointed Field Director of the joint Egypt Exploration Society and Leiden Museum expedition at Saqqara. He is the author of monographs on Egyptian administrative seals, the tomb of Akhenaten at El-Amarna, reliefs and inscriptions from Saqqara, the Sacred Animal Necropolis at Saqqara, the Memphite tomb of Horemheb and Ramesside tombs at Saqqara. Plates 57, 60-66.

Hilary Weir, M.A. She lived in Cairo from 1979 to 1985 while her husband was British Ambassador to Egypt. Her principal interest during those years was post-pharaonic Egyptian history, both Coptic and Islamic, on which she wrote a number of articles and a booklet, *Medieval Cairo - A Visitor's Guide*. As Secretary and Treasurer of the Society for the Preservation of the Architectural Resources of Egypt she was active in the campaign to overcome the growing threat to Cairo's heritage of Islamic and other monuments. She has now resumed her career in the British diplomatic service and works in the Foreign and Commonwealth Office in London. Plates 75-124.

Charles Newton, B.A., A.M.A. A research assistant in the Department of Design, Prints and Drawings at the Victoria & Albert Museum, he has a wide range of interests. He is the author or co-author of books and exhibition catalogues as diverse in subject as Photography in Printmaking, British textile design, and the work of the painter Amadei, Count Preziosi. He is largely responsible for integrating the Searight Collection of pictures of the Middle East into the collection of the V & A and is particularly interested in the work of J.F. Lewis. He has specialised in identifying topographical views of Turkey by European artists. Plates 125-173.

Francis Maddison, M.A., F.S.A. A Fellow of Linacre College, Oxford, and Corresponding Member of the Académie internationale de l'Histoire des Science, he is also a founding member of the Société internationale de l'Astrolabe. He has been Curator of the Museum of the History of Science, Oxford, since 1964. He has published widely on the history of European and Islamic early scientific and navigational instruments, horology, and some wider historical subjects. He is co-author with the late Alain Brieux of *Répertoire des facteurs d'astrolabes et de leurs oeuvres,* 1ère partie, 'Islam, plus Byzance, Arménie, Géorgie et Inde hindoue'. Plate 174.

Napoleon's invasion of Egypt in 1798 was a romantic alternative to an invasion of Britain. He landed at Alexandria on 1 July and took up his quarters by 'Pompey's Pillar' (pl. 71). Much of the army became ill from eating watermelons, but within three weeks Napoleon had taken Cairo and won a battle against the Mameluke rulers of Egypt. He had addressed the army on the subject of the 40 centuries that looked down on them from the pyramids of Giza and was now established in the capital. The riches of the country astonished him; he was less complimentary about its population. His curiosity and zeal for administrative reform were insatiable. Egypt responded generously to the former but was recalcitrant towards the latter. On 1 August 1798 Nelson destroyed the French fleet, and from that moment Napoleon had lost his Egyptian gamble. But he was never lacking in resource. He declared to the local population that the French were true Moslems; he planned the conquest of the whole country as far south as Aswan; his military ambition took him beyond Egypt to Palestine, where Acre under Sir Sydney Smith held out against him. Smith reported that the plain of Nazareth had proved the boundary of Napoleon's remarkable career. This was not so, for Waterloo was 16 years away.

Napoleon's sense of history suggested to him that the monuments of science might be more enduring than the monuments of war. To accompany the Egyptian expedition he formed a Commission of Arts and Science, which was to investigate all aspects of Egypt, ancient and modern. The Commission had 165 members, not all of whom would return to France at the end of the campaign. Napoleon's enthusiasm for this side of his venture was demonstrated during the journey to Egypt, when he participated in many shipboard debates on matters religious, political and scientific. His model, as in much else, may have been Alexander the Great, who also marched with savants in attendance. There was a precedent too, unknown to Napoleon, in Egypt itself, where Tuthmosis III of the 18th dynasty left in the temple of Karnak a zoological and botanical record of his third campaign to Syria and Palestine. The largest sections of the Commission were concerned with civil engineering, surveying and mapping. But there were gifted architects and artists in abundance. Napoleon had wanted the composer Méhul to come too, pleased by his opera on the crossing of the bridge at Lodi; but Méhul preferred Paris to Cairo.

The spearhead of Napoleon's scientific plans was the Institute of Egypt, founded on 22 August 1798. Bonaparte himself was vice-president and was numbered among the 12 mathematicians. The other sections were concerned with physics, political economy, literature and art. The Institute held its meetings in a splendid Cairo house (pl. 98) vacated by its owner, who fought the French in Upper Egypt. The objects of the Institute were to propagate the sciences in Egypt; to gather and publish natural, industrial and historical data on Egypt; and to assist the government in any matter it might wish to investigate. Napoleon was indefatigable in posing questions to the Institute, about growing wine in Egypt, building a canal across the isthmus of Suez, digging wells in the desert, constructing windmills. If his own concerns were practical, the savants had their opportunity to research far into the mysterious land of Egypt. If the army was sometimes at a loss to know what it was doing in Egypt, the scientists were in their element. To the store-rooms of the Institute were gathered over a period of three years the materials for the monumental *Description de l'Egypte*, the first edition of which was to contain 10 volumes of text and 13 of plates, appearing in instalments from 1809.

Three days after the foundation of the Institute, General Desaix was ready to launch a campaign into Upper Egypt on Napoleon's behalf. The main quarry was the Mameluke Murad Bey, who lured the army ever deeper to the south, evading constantly, and managing to levy taxes always just ahead of the French. Murad's tactics eventually returned Desaix to his starting point, Cairo. With Desaix's expedition went Vivant Denon, a member of the Institute and future director of the Louvre. With the engineers Duvilliers and Jollois he was the first of the savants to see the full glory of Egypt's past. He was entirely at the mercy of military vicissitudes, but managed to produce a magnificent series of temple drawings in Upper Egypt. The drawings were made initially with the drawing-board resting on his knee, or when standing, or when on horseback. He responded with justifiable pride when the French army presented arms in awe at the first sight of Thebes. Denon's account of Egypt was published separately in 1802, but his pioneering efforts fired the Institute and Commission towards their ultimate goal of the *Description*. In the summer of 1799 Napoleon decided that glory might be more readily available in

Europe than in Egypt. He departed on 22 August with a handful of followers, including Denon. One of his last acts in Egypt was to decree for the Commission a scientific expedition southwards.

Every effort had been made to conquer Egypt; every effort was now made to describe it. A provisional scheme for the *Description* was established. The marvels of Egyptian antiquity would predominate; detailed maps of Egypt would be the centrepiece; modern Egypt would be covered through its buildings, its arts and crafts, and the dress of its people; the geology, flora and fauna would also be represented. The gathering of material for 900 plates was no mean feat, and its delineation was divided among a large number of artists. The most gifted of them was probably the painter Dutertre, who was responsible not only for the shrewd portraits of Murad, the Abyssinian bishop, the poet and the astronomer (pls. 157, 165, 158, 159), but also for such fine landscapes as the two scenes of Philae (pls. 1 - 2), the statue in the forecourt of Karnak (pl. 21), and the general views of Asyut, Minya, Ezbekiya Square in Cairo and the Hakim mosque (pls. 45, 119, 94, 80). He addressed the Institute on the problems of setting up a school of fine arts in Egypt. Equally imposing in their way are imaginative reconstructions of the temples of Kom Ombo, Esna, Contralatopolis and Dendera (pls. 6, 12 - 14, 38) attempted by the engineers Duvilliers and Jollois. These men went originally to Upper Egypt to report on irrigation and make suggestions for its improvement. Most of the drawings for the arts and crafts section (pls. 125 - 156) were done by Jacques-Nicolas Conté, who was the mechanical brain behind the Commission and later proposed the use of balloons for an invasion of Britain. Apart from producing surgical instruments and microscope lenses when required, he manufactured for the Commission a constant supply of pencils.

The majority of the Commission left Egypt in September 1801 after the military capitulation to the British. Such was the devotion of the scientists to their collections of birds, animals, reptiles, plants and rocks that they declared that they would follow them to England rather than be parted from them. The collections were ceded to France; but the British Museum acquired impressive additions to its Egyptian holding, and most notably the Rosetta Stone (pls. 72-74). In France the body responsible for the eventual publishing of the *Description* was presided over by the chemist Claude-Louis Berthollet. He had recruited many of the scholars for the Egyptian venture but had left for France with Napoleon in August 1799. The staggering task of coordinating the work was undertaken initially by the same Lancret who had first informed the Institute about the discovery of the Rosetta Stone. After his death it was Edmé-François Jomard who supervised the organisation and production of the *Description*. Jomard had been only 20 when the expedition sailed. He contributed plates to the *Description*, notably of Antinoopolis, Beni Hasan and the Fayum (pls. 49, 54 - 57). More importantly, he undertook the detailed writing up of most of the monuments from the First Cataract to Cairo (with the main exceptions of Philae, Esna and Thebes). He supplied also a number of learned excursuses.

The preparation of the *Description* was a remarkable achievement, worthy of the splendours it enshrined. Some 400 engravers worked on the task, and roughly 2000 people were involved each year in the furtherance of the project. Special paper was used, and the eventual publication was without parallel in the annals of historical research. The fame of the *Description* spread quickly throughout Europe, but knowledge of it was confined to a few. The first edition was little circulated among the French themselves. Despite the immense labour involved, Louis XVIII decreed in 1820 that a second revised edition should be embarked on, for the financial benefit of those who had undertaken the original research, for the furtherance of the fine arts, and the development of the craft of engraving. Impressions were again taken of the 900 plates.

The first edition was still incomplete in 1822, the year Jean-François Champollion published his discoveries about hieroglyphic writing. Jomard opposed his theories and remained a steadfast enemy throughout Champollion's career. The value of the *Description* towards hieroglyphic decipherment was limited, because the ancient texts had been copied in ignorance and often with a speed that impaired accuracy. When Champollion went to Egypt in 1828, exactly 30 years after Napoleon, he worked with the fervour and assurance of exact knowledge. Yet it was the devoted savants of the *Description* who, with their determination to record all they saw as best they could, first brought Egypt within the range of modern science, and left behind a record of her condition at the turn of the 18th and 19th centuries that could only stimulate further research.

ROBERT ANDERSON

ANCIENT EGYPT

When Vivant Denon saw briefly the giant portico at Hermopolis (pl. 48), he considered it the first monument to reveal to him the architecture of ancient Egypt and that it had been awaiting him for 4,000 years. He was not to know that the portico was built by Alexander the Great and Philip Arrhidaeus towards the end of the 4th century B.C.; still less that in 1822 the building would be finally demolished. An important aspect of the Commission's work was the record of monuments that were not to survive the 19th century. Sometimes later scholars, equipped with a knowledge beyond that of the Commission and not pressed by the exigencies of a military operation, described these antiquities before they disappeared. This was so with the temple of Amenophis III on Elephantine (pls. 3 and 4), the Ptolemaic shrine north of Esna (pl. 13), Cleopatra's building at Armant (pls. 15 - 17), and the scenes from the town enclosure east of Dendera (pl. 40). But without the pioneer work of the *Description*, much information would be lacking on the ruins of Contralatopolis (pl. 14), the lofty columns by the Nile at Antaeopolis (pls. 42, 43), certain aspects of the tombs at Asyut (pls. 46, 47), Alexander's portico at Hermopolis (pl. 48), the standing monuments of Hadrian's Antinoopolis (pls. 49 - 53), and the so-called Roman tower at Alexandria (pl. 69). These ruins were swept away by an Egypt emerging into the modern world and impatient of its past.

When seen by the French, the monuments were still cumbered by the deposits of many ages. The double shrine at Kom Ombo (pl. 5), was almost engulfed by the sand, its multifarious plant capitals emerging as tantalising hints of what might be below. The roof of the Edfu temple had become a modern village (pl. 8), crawling with children and animals. The obelisks at Luxor (pl. 18) — one of them had not yet made the journey to Paris — had their pedestals obscured, and entry to the temple was at the level of Abu el-Haggag's mosque. Columns of the first courtyard had been divided up among the villagers; there was good stabling between them, and they provided pleasant shade for a school. The massive lion-body of the Sphinx at Giza was visible in its hinder parts, but the front was obscured (pl. 65); nothing could be seen of the stela between its paws on which the Sphinx was supposed to address the young Tuthmosis IV in a dream and beg that even in the 15th century B.C. the surrounding sand should be removed.

Though no scientific excavation was attempted, some clearance might be undertaken if time allowed. At Dendera, for instance, much work had to be done before the bases of the columns could be measured and the full height of the hypostyle hall appreciated (pl. 38). The time spent clearing the exterior back wall at Dendera gave less opportunity to copy texts. Cleopatra the Great and Caesarion were revealed, but their cartouches were left blank (pl. 37). In the Ramesseum, the vivid siege of the Syrian fortress Dapur was copied with haste (pl. 31). It had to be included for its intrinsic interest; but many details were omitted, and the artist confessed he was unable to place the scene in context, with Ramesses II himself menacing from his chariot to the left. Countless figures were copied, human and divine, but rarely did the French artists approximate to the Egyptian canon of proportion that gave the originals their dignity and poise. The pyramids between the Fayum and Giza were treated so sketchily it is difficult to tell which monument was being drawn. The drawings were actually done from the Nile some miles away, time preventing any nearer approach.

The sense of wonder felt by the French artists is manifest. The scale of the buildings was a constant astonishment to the Commission. The vast extent of Karnak was awesome beyond all other sites (pls. 19 - 27). Nothing in Greece could compare with it, unless the temple of Olympian Zeus at Athens. What of Palmyra and Baalbeck, ruins well-known to 18th-century Europe? Not even St. Peter's in modern Rome or the ancient Roman forums could compare. Only Versailles, the French thought, and the combination of the Louvre and the Tuileries, with all the monuments that might eventually adorn them, could rival Karnak.

Imagination and acute observation gave dramatic atmosphere to the Ptolemaic temple at Qasr Qarun as seen by moonlight (pl. 56). Similarly evocative are the Giza pyramids at sunrise (pl. 60), and the flaming torches within the Grand Gallery of the Cheops pyramid (pl. 62). The conjectural restorations may have more panache than accuracy. As an impression of what Egyptian majesty meant to these intelligent European observers, they are endlessly stimulating. It hardly mattered that insufficient clearance at Kom Ombo caused the structures of the forecourt and the ancient entrance to the temple to be omitted (pl. 6). The Taharqa colonnade in the first court at Karnak, represented by only one standing column then as now, is restored beyond its original splendour (pl.

26), with 12 columns instead of the requisite 10. Likewise the temple at Antaeopolis, complete with admiring priests, has been given a façade without intercolumnar walls. The French artist has given the shrine, so soon to fall victim to the undermining waters of the Nile, six entrances too many (pl. 44). No Egyptian temple could ever be so open to the public eye; yet the two previous plates give the evidence for his inspiration.

Many of the scenes show a quick eye for detail. At an opposite extreme from the violent action captured at the siege of Dapur (pl. 31) is the calm intensity of the two harp players from the tomb of Ramesses III (pl. 34). The Commissioners made the point that James Bruce, who first copied the scene in 1768, had produced inaccurate results. That they did likewise does not detract from the improvement they effected in our knowledge. There was evident delight taken in the giraffe at Armant (pl. 17), and in the desert hunting scene at Beni Hasan (pl. 55). There too, the French artist was fascinated by the scene of a man being bastinadoed at a counting of the oxen. In the tombs near the Second Pyramid at Giza, the vitality of the boat building scene caught the eye, as did the man suspended horizontally as part of a human winepress (pl. 66). Such was the enthusiasm of those commissioners who first saw the tomb scenes at El-Kab that they urged others who had gone on to Esna to return immediately; this they did in the middle of the night.

The detailed site descriptions that accompanied the Commissioners' plates inevitably contained errors of interpretation. The authors did not realise that some of the most imposing monuments they had seen were built since the time of Alexander the Great. They allowed only 1663 years for pharaonic history before the Persian conqueror, Cambyses (525 B.C.). The antiquity of a structure was deduced from signs of weathering on the stone or the level of accomplishment in its working. Thus the temple of Isis on Philae (pl. 2) was assumed to be pre-Persian rather than mainly Ptolemaic, the texts of Edfu suggested that the temple had been built to celebrate the start of a Sothic cycle, the date on which, after 1460 years, the civil and astronomical calendars of ancient Egypt coincided again; the Roman temple of Esna must be earlier still as the carving seemed less developed and the workmanship was more crude. An erroneous distinction was made between temples covered with religious scenes and those, such as Luxor, Karnak, and Medinet Habu, that were more concerned with notable battles; the latter were thought to be palaces. Thus the palace of Medinet Habu was associated with the Sesostris of Herodotus because of the extensive conquests recorded; in fact they were largely grandiloquent imitations of scenes at the Ramesseum. In spite of the Tiberius inscription in Greek on the façade at Dendera, it was unthinkable that so grand a building should be Roman and belong to a period of religious decadence.

Many of these errors arose through a too great reliance on classical authors. This was inevitable without a knowledge of hieroglyphs. Much admiration was expressed for the superb carvings on the granite obelisks of Luxor, and it was realised that the frequent repetition of sign groups there might aid eventual decipherment of the language. Yet the hieroglyphic copies made by the Commission have many faults. It is not just that signs were distorted because their proper forms were not understood. The layout of the hieroglyphs copied has none of the systematic elegance displayed by the originals; and even the cartouches are often bungled. A main reason for this was the fact that most of the texts copied came from Graeco-Roman temples, where individual signs and their grouping had lost the finesse of earlier times.

But when the discovery of the Rosetta Stone was announced to the Institute on 19 July 1799, its significance was immediately recognised. This monument was to be the crown of all the antiquities collected in Cairo by the Commission. There was the magnificent granite fist of Ramesses II found at Memphis (pl. 59); the basalt obelisks dedicated to the ibis-god Thoth and adorning a Cairo mosque (pl. 68); the huge sarcophagus of Nectanebo II used as an ablution tank in a mosque at Alexandria (pl. 70). A new zeal for the copying of inscriptions was provided by the find at Rosetta. The scholars were tireless in their attempts to record as many as they could of the texts they found on stone or papyrus. When the antiquities were eventually ceded to the British, the French had copies and squeezes adequate to the pursuance of their labours. Yet when the Rosetta Stone came to publication in the *Description* (pls. 72-74), a special journey was made to London so as to consult the original in the British Museum. It was only right that it should be a Frenchman, Jean-François Champollion, who published in 1822, the year that the Commission completed the 'Antiquités' section of the first edition of the *Description*, the initial giant strides in the decipherment of the ancient Egyptian language.

ROBERT ANDERSON

12

The monuments of Philae are here seen from the north-east. The island lies to the south of Aswan and the first cataract. This was the furthest the French expedition penetrated on the Nile. The presence of the army is commemorated by an inscription on the first pylon of the Isis temple. In the foreground on the island is the gateway of the Roman emperor Diocletian; to the right is the Ptolemaic Isis temple; to the left is the kiosk of Trajan. The granite rocks on the island of Bigah, sacred to Osiris, fill the right background. In the foreground French soldiers escort a laden camel. With the building of the old Aswan dam in 1899, the monuments of Philae came under threat, being partially submerged each year. The construction of the High Dam was decisive for the future of the island. The monuments were now to be permanently submerged, and the decision was taken to remove them stone by stone to the neighbouring island of Agelkia, where they have since been reassembled. By blasting and considerable engineering works, the shape of Agelkia has been made to resemble that of Philae as much as possible.

The great temple of Isis and kiosk of Trajan from the south-west. The background shows the rugged nature of the local granite outcrops. Though the entrance gate to the temple was built by Nectanebo I of the 30th dynasty, one of the last native rulers of pharaonic Egypt, the bulk of the temple is Ptolemaic. It was started by Ptolemy II Philadelphus, in whose reign the Pharos of Alexandria was constructed. On the first pylon is Ptolemy XII, father of Cleopatra the Great, in a symbolic scene of clubbing the enemies he left Rome to fight. Much of the exterior decoration is by the Roman emperors Augustus and Tiberius. The kiosk of Trajan was left incomplete, with some capitals partially carved, and only a few interior reliefs fully worked. The worship of Isis continued here into the reign of Justinian in the 6th century A.D., when the temples were finally closed, the priests dispossessed, and the images taken to Constantinople. Many brick structures can be seen; these have since been cleared from the site. French scholars are portrayed at work on the mapping and description of the island.

PLATE 3

TEMPLE ON ELEPHANTINE

T he small 18th-dynasty temple built by Amenophis III on the island of Elephantine no longer exists. It was destroyed in 1822. It was dedicated to Khnum, the ram-headed god of the first cataract who controlled the floodwaters of Egypt. The temple lay to the north-west of the Nilometer, which still exists and was used to measure the height of the inundation. The columns at the front of the temple, representing papyrus buds, are similar to those in the colonnaded court at Luxor built by the same king. The blocks in front of the shrine are the scattered remains of a monumental staircase, and to the right is an unfinished seated statue, probably of Osiris. A winged disk surmounts the façade, and within the portico is a representation of the king before Khnum. The Greek name Elephantine is a translation of the ancient word for ivory, which commemorates the former trade of the island.

PLATE 4   SCENES FROM TEMPLE ON ELEPHANTINE

Two scenes from the destroyed temple of Amenophis III on the island of Elephantine. Both scenes formed part of the temple sanctuary, the upper one on the outside, the lower having adorned one of the interior walls. The original commentary regrets that the hieroglyphs of the upper scene could not be copied for lack of time, whereas those of the other scene have been precisely drawn. The main gods depicted are those of the first cataract, who formed a triad. The ram-headed Khnum appears three times; his consort Anukis, with high feathered headdress, and Satis, wearing the white crown of Upper Egypt with antelope horns, are shown twice. The upper scene has in addition an unnamed goddess on the left and an ithyphallic Amun-Re on the right. The upper scene shows a coronation of Amenophis and three varieties of offering. In the scene below Amenophis III and Queen Tiye with an arched sistrum or temple rattle are offering to the ram-headed boat of Khnum, while Satis presents the king to the god himself.

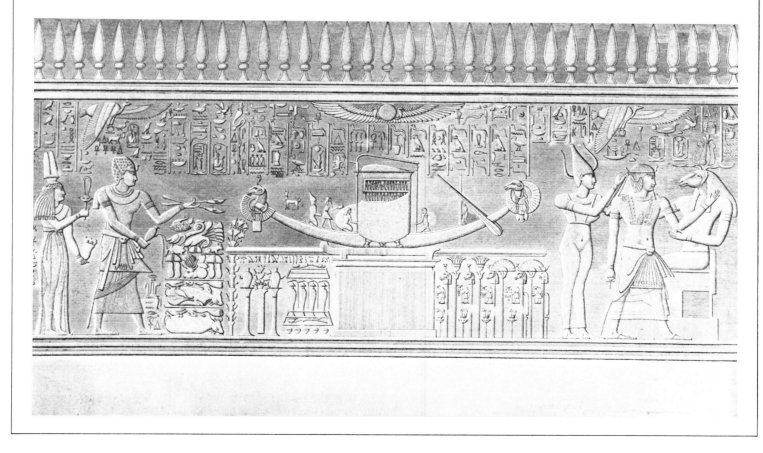

At the time of the French expedition the temple of Kom Ombo was largely obscured by rubble and sand. The outer hypostyle hall, decorated by Ptolemy XII, is the main feature of the plate. The elaborate plant capitals, characteristic of a Ptolemaic temple, are clearly shown. The two winged disks, sacred emblem of the god Horus, mark the main axes of what is in fact a double temple with two sanctuaries. The area to the left is dedicated to Haroeris, the Greek name of the hawk god, Horus the elder; the other part is dedicated to the crocodile god, Sobek. The inner hypostyle hall of Ptolemy VI is hardly visible above the sand. A French soldier is patrolling the background, one of the artists approaches the temple, and a meal is being cooked above the dunes. The massive masonry of the fallen blocks gives some impression of the engineering prowess shown by the original builders and of the problems faced by the restorers of the temple.

PLATE 6   TEMPLE OF KOM OMBO

An imaginative reconstruction of the Ptolemaic temple of Kom Ombo. In the foreground is the Nile, which over the centuries has eroded the banks and caused much havoc to the temple. To the right is the great gateway of Ptolemy XII, through which the visitor now enters the temple complex; the nearer wing of this gate has been washed away by the river. To the left is the Birth House of Ptolemy VI, with capitals representing the head of Hathor, goddess of love and music. The artist has clearly shown the double nature of the temple by means of the two giant porticoes. The imposing brick enclosure wall appears at what may have been its original height. The scenes on the façade of the hypostyle hall are largely imaginary, as they were mostly invisible at the time beneath the covering of sand. The French artists could not know that the forecourt of the temple, here shown bare, had columns round it decorated by the Roman emperor Tiberius, and that the ancient entrance to the temple had already fallen prey to the river in the immediate foreground. The scene is as if depicted, so the commentary tells us, from a boat at anchor in the Nile with the inundation waters at their height.

PLATE 7

GEBEL ES-SILSILA

G ebel es-Silsila is the modern name of the quarry area from which came much of the sandstone used in the building of Upper Egyptian temples. Quarrying was carried out on both sides of the river, but the scene shows a group of rock shrines and monumental inscriptions from the west bank. On the right is the capstan-shaped rock that has given its name to the site, the 'mountain of the chain', and legend has it that a chain was thrown across the river from this rock for the purpose of exacting dues from passing ships. The rock inscription partially obscured by the houseboat is in honour of Ramesses III. The shrines to the left belong to Merneptah and Ramesses II, and the badly damaged one on the extreme left was set up by Sethos I. The area behind the shrines has been largely cut away by the quarry workers, whose precision and skill is well attested by the clean-cut vertical faces they have left behind them in the rock. The houseboat has been commandeered for the occasion by the French.

With the Arabian desert hills and the Nile as background, the artist has given a vivid impression of the Ptolemaic temple at Edfu before its excavation. Sand obscures much of the building; debris mounts up the columns of the hypostyle hall; houses of the village, with characteristic pigeon towers, are built against the first pylon; and even the roof of the temple has been used for a jumble of dwellings. Yet much of the grandeur survives, for Edfu is the most complete of all Egyptian temples. On the nearer wing of the pylon are various scenes of Ptolemy XII before gods. In the top register he offers an image of Maat, goddess of truth; in the second he offers a headband; and at the bottom he appears beneath a winged vulture in giant form clubbing his enemies before Horus of Edfu and Hathor of Dendera. In the foreground is a Mameluke tent. Outside it the French artist greets a local horseman, while on the other side a servant holds his weapons of war.

PLATE 9

HYPOSTYLE HALL AT EDFU

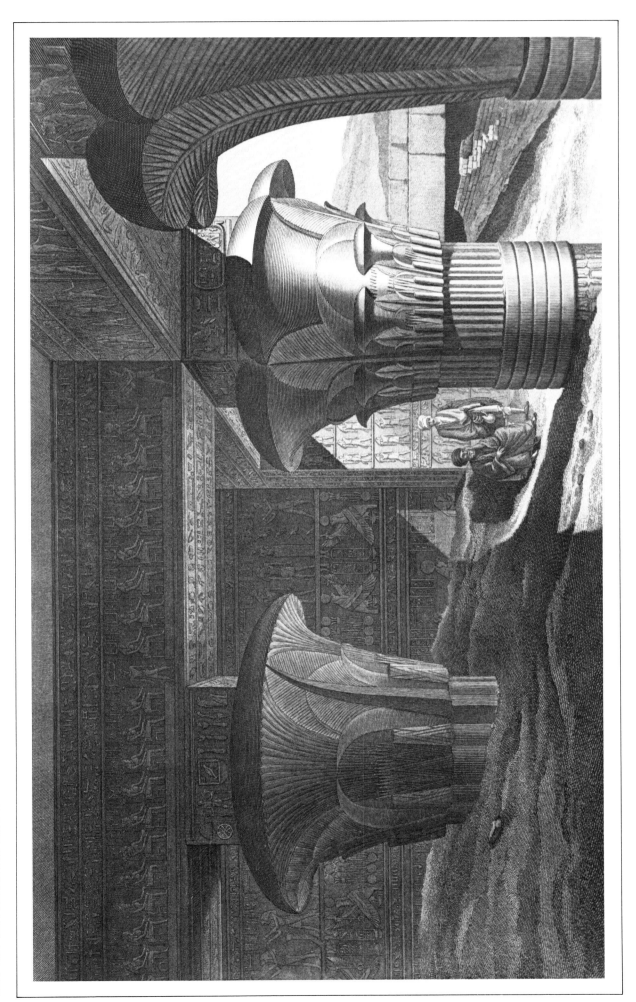

T he temple of Edfu was begun under Ptolemy III and its decoration completed under Ptolemy XII. It was 180 years in the building. The outer hypostyle hall was decorated by Ptolemy VI; the two composite plant capitals combine many motifs from earlier periods, and the elegant palm-leaf capital is especially characteristic of the Ptolemaic architects. The hall is shown cumbered with debris at a time when a thriving village community had houses at the walls of the temple and even on its roof. On the architrave the king offers to the sun-god Re and to seven of his divine emanations, with a further ten deities beyond. On the facing wall the royal cartouches are protected by winged hawks. The brick structure to the right has been removed and the temple completely cleared. It is now known that the temple walls preserve some of the most ancient and important mythological texts from ancient Egypt. The two local inhabitants wear the Turkish fashion of the period.

21

PLATE 10   BIRTH HOUSE AT EDFU

For this reconstruction of the Birth House at Edfu the artist has imagined the shrine completely excavated, with all the encroaching sand removed. At the same time he has removed the court through which the building was approached and which still contains scenes of music being played on harp and lute. The floral capitals are surmounted by figures of the dwarf-god Bes, shown naked. Bes was associated with life in the home and was a helper to women in childbirth. The temple celebrated the divine birth of Ptolemy VI. Within the sanctuary Khnum is depicted moulding him on a potter's wheel along with the divine child Harsomtus. The king's good fortune is assured by seven Hathors with tambourines. The exterior decoration was completed under Ptolemy IX. The scenes shown here are a conflation of what had been copied from other Egyptian birth houses. The large scenes on the façade have in fact since been destroyed. Those on the side wall represent Ptolemy VI before various deities. The slight incline towards the temple and its ancient visitors have been invented by the artist.

T he tomb of Paheri at El-Kab, on the east bank of the Nile between Edfu and Esna, commemorates one of
the most distinguished families of the early 18th dynasty. His grandfather Ahmose was present at the siege
of Avaris, capital of the foreign Hyksos rulers in the Delta; he campaigned also into Nubia under
Amenophis I and again under Tuthmosis I, who took him north on an expedition across the Euphrates into
Naharin. Paheri himself was count of El-Kab and of Esna, some 22 miles to the north; he was responsible for the
corn accounts from Dendera to El-Kab; and he was superintendant of priests of the local vulture goddess Nekhbet.
His is the central figure at the back of the tomb niche. His wife Henuterneheh is behind the artist at work on the
scene, while his mother Kem is on Paheri's other side. On one of the walls of the niche Paheri makes offering to two
royal children, thus indicating the family's close connection with the reigning house. A long inscription covers the
façade of the niche: in it Paheri propounds his virtues, prays for a blessed future, and implores visitors to repeat the
formulas necessary to ensure his food supply.

PLATE 12   TEMPLE OF ESNA

The temple of Esna lies well below the level of the modern city. Dedicated to the ram-headed Khnum as chief god, it was built in Ptolemaic and Roman times. Hardly more than the hypostyle hall, with its 18 plant columns, survives. The area to the left, surmounted by a cavetto cornice, dates to Ptolemy VI; the rest of the hall is Roman, with cartouches of such emperors as Domitian, Trajan and Hadrian. The latest of all Roman cartouches, that of Decius (A.D. 249-251), appears here. An astronomical ceiling with signs of the zodiac is represented at the top of the plate. The artist has shown a religious procession entering the temple, with a lavishly decked ram near the front. Texts on the columns tell us much more about the festivals of ancient Esna, when the statue of Khnum was brought from the sanctuary for such celebrations as the Raising of the Heavens or Setting-up the Potter's Wheel. The allusive writing system used here produces 143 different ways of representing Khnum's name in hieroglyphs.

The North Temple of Khnum, once situated near Esna, has completely disappeared. The French artist has given an imaginative reconstruction of the considerable ruins visible to the expedition. The temple was Ptolemaic; the façade was restored by Ptolemy III, the columns had cartouches of Ptolemy V. Trajan's name occurred in the temple, and one of its features was a fine astronomical ceiling. The temple stood about two and a half miles to the northwest of the main city. Texts in the hypostyle hall at Esna explain that the young god Heka, the rejuvenated form of older gods and in whose person vegetation revived, would be received with rejoicing after procession to the North Temple. He would be greeted in terms suitable to a king returning in victory from foreign parts. Heka should arrive 'like the inundation, to nourish the Two Lands, to give life to all types of men'.

PLATE 14   TEMPLE OF CONTRALATOPOLIS

The Ptolemaic and Roman temple of Contralatopolis, the modern El-Hilla, lay opposite Esna on the east bank of the Nile. It was dedicated to Isis and was completely destroyed in 1828. But at the time of the French expedition there was sufficient evidence for the artist to attempt a conjectural reconstruction of the temple. The Hathor columns were said to be less finely worked than those at Dendera or Philae, and much of the decoration was unfinished. The plan of the temple seemed bizarre, since the rooms at the back were not regularly grouped round the axis of the temple. Above the entrance can be seen the bark of the beetle-god, Khepri. The cartouches on the façade have not been filled in, but we know that that of the Roman emperor Antoninus Pius was among them. The temple may have been started by Ptolemy IX, since it was his cartouche that appeared on the entrance to the inner hall. The scenes between the columns bear little resemblance to those appearing later in the notes of the English scholar, J. Gardner Wilkinson. The French artist used his imagination, as with the figures standing in the temple entrance.

This temple, on the west bank of the Nile at Armant, was dedicated to the war-god Montu and his consort Rat-tawy. It no longer exists. It was built at the end of the Ptolemaic period by Cleopatra the Great and Caesarion, her son supposedly by Julius Caesar. The columns are more slender for their height than was usual in ancient Egypt. The view is taken from the south-west and shows the seven columns that continued to stand through much of the 19th century. The nearest column had a scene of Caesarion with Ptah, and the other six had representations of Cleopatra and her son in front of local gods and other deities. With the destruction of this temple, the only surviving scene of Cleopatra and Caesarion is at Dendera. The artist has shown a large domed tomb of a sheikh built against the walls of the temple, and a number of other Moslem graves. A pair of Frenchmen is inspecting the temple with a view to recording it; another draughtsman is already at work behind the sheikh's tomb. Their servants are with them, and two soldiers patrol the roof of the temple.

PLATE 16   TEMPLE OF ARMANT

V iew from the west of the destroyed temple to Montu and Rat-tawy at Armant. The blocks in the forecourt are the remains of columns and screen-walls. On the column immediately in front of the main temple, where a soldier can be seen mounting guard, was a scene of Cleopatra holding a pair of sistra before Rat-tawy. The lintel of the main temple had a double scene of Rat-tawy suckling a child; behind her in both cases was Meskhenet, goddess of the birth chamber, of the birth stool and the birth stones; Hathor likewise appeared twice with a tambourine, and behind her was Cleopatra holding the two types of Egyptian sistrum, one in the form of a small shrine, the other arched. This is the instrument Virgil describes her as rattling at the battle of Actium in 31 B.C. Caesarion in attitude of adoration followed his mother in both scenes. On the north wall of the temple Caesarion appeared before the model of a sacred cow, and Cleopatra was shown worshipping Bukhis, the local bull supposed to be the incarnation of the war-god Montu and the colour of whose hair was said to change every hour.

These eight scenes all come from the destroyed temple of Armant built by Cleopatra the Great and Caesarion. Nos. 1-3, 5-6 and 8 were in the inner hall of the temple. No. 1 depicts Harpocrates on a lotus before Hathor, with Nephthys behind him; nos. 2 and 6 are mystical scenes, with the dwarf god Bes and hippopotamus Thoeris prominent in the latter; no. 3 shows Rat-tawy suckling a child, with Isis and a lion-headed Satis behind; no. 5 has the ibis-god Thoth offering to a cat, probably that of Heliopolis; the upper part of no. 8 shows a winged hawk in a clump of lotus adored by Isis and Nephthys (the artist has depicted two figures of Nephthys in error), with Bes and an ithyphallic Amun-Re to the left, Thoeris and Ptah to the right; the lintel in scene 8 again shows Harpocrates on a lotus facing another Harpocrates carried between the horns of a cow, with suckling goddesses framed by a winged goddess at either end. Scene 4, showing a cat and uraeus on shrines, comes from the temple staircase. Scene 7, depicting a giraffe, was on the back wall of the temple.

PLATE 18

T his plate presents a view of the façade of the temple of Luxor, which, like that of Karnak two miles distant to the north, was dedicated to the great Theban deity Amun-Re. The condition of the temple depicted here, encumbered as it is with the dwellings, pigeon cotes and a mosque of a thriving community, persisted to some extent up to the Second World War, although the mounds of debris inside the temple had been cleared in the late 19th century. Now the whole façade is cleared and it is evident to the visitor today that originally the great gateway was embellished with two obelisks, four standing colossi and two seated colossi, all of Ramesses II. Only one of the standing colossi is still in position. Ramesses had added the pylon and the huge court behind it to the original temple built by Amenophis III and extended by Tutankhamun and Horemheb. The reliefs on the outside of the pylon show episodes from the momentous battle fought at Kadesh in Syria between the Egyptians and the Hittites in Ramesses's fifth regnal year. Although it was celebrated as a famous victory by Ramesses, it was clearly a close run thing from which both sides were probably content to disengage. The obelisk on the right was taken down in 1836, and now distinguishes the Place de la Concorde in Paris.

PLATE 19

TEMPLE OF KARNAK

T he remains of the various temple structures which make up the complex of Karnak occupy an area of more than 60 acres, a divine temenos of unparalleled size surrounded by a massive wall of mud-brick. Such are the size and variety of the buildings that the French scholars of Napoleon's expedition could only conceive them as the remains of a huge palace. In a sense they were right, for an Egyptian temple was the 'mansion of the god', his earthly home where, in the form of his divine image, he lived, ate, drank, was clothed and was worshipped by the king and his priestly assistants. This panoramic view of the temple comprises all the most important parts of the complex as they could be seen in the last years of the 18th century. On the right is the main temple building with the earliest parts, of 18th dynasty date, lying nearest to the observer. The obelisk is the sole survivor of a pair set up by Queen Hatshepsut before what is now known as the fifth pylon of the main temple of Amun-Re. It is 97ft high. The buildings on the left form part of the extension to the main temple which led to the south enclosure wall, a series of courts and pylons begun in the 18th dynasty, but now largely ruined.

PLATE 20   FIRST COURT AND HYPOSTYLE HALL AT KARNAK

When Karnak was visited by French scholars in the late 18th century, it was found to be a veritable shambles of vast structures, reduced to the condition of a romantic ruin on the grandest scale – the result of years of natural decay and of human pillaging. Not until quite late in the 19th century were serious efforts made to rebuild what could still be restored to a semblance of its former glory, and to repair even more destruction brought about by earth-tremors. The ancient Egyptian architects never appreciated the importance of good foundations. The visitor to Karnak today enters the great temple complex through the huge first pylon built in the Late Period (possibly the 30th dynasty), and faces, more or less precisely, the view shown here. The piles of rubble which lie to left and right of the monumental entrance to the hypostyle hall (glimpsed in the background), represent the second pylon. These piles have now been largely reassembled and are happily much more recognisable as the formal double gate which once formed the east side of the first court. The single surviving column of the Taharqa colonnade in the centre of the scene was itself taken down and rebuilt for reasons of safety in 1928-9.

The viewing point of this plate lies at the entrance to the vestibule leading to the great hypostyle hall of the Karnak temple looking south. To the right can be seen part of the small pylon front of the temple built by Ramesses III of the 20th dynasty, which at the time of its construction lay outside the main temple area of Karnak. Just to the left of this temple-within-a-temple, and behind the colossal sculpture is the Bubastite portal, so called because it is heavily inscribed with important texts carved in the 22nd dynasty, the kings of which stemmed from the city of Bubastis in the Delta. The central feature of the plate is the granite colossus which stands at the side of the vestibule, here contemplated by one of the scholars who accompanied Napoleon's expedition, dressed more appropriately for the Paris winter than for any Egyptian season. This huge statue, which can now be seen with its head replaced, represents Ramesses II, the great builder, whose sculptured image dominates so many of the surviving Egyptian monuments. On the sides of the lower part of the colossus are sunk relief figures of the princess Bint-Anath, who became one of Ramesses's principal wives in the later years of his reign.

PLATE 22   RAM-HEADED SPHINXES AT KARNAK

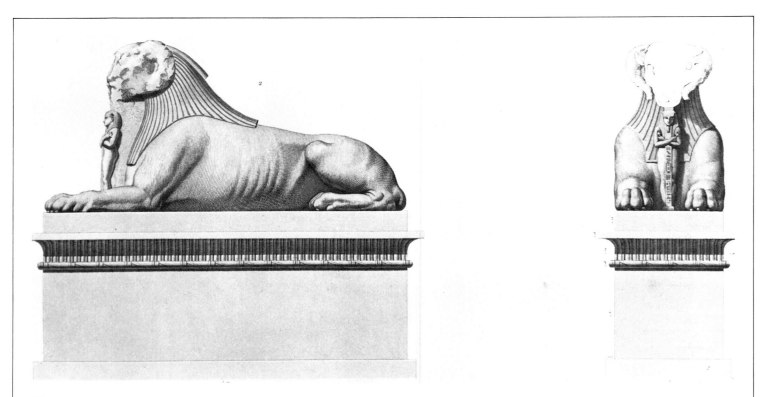

The common approach to a great temple was by an avenue lined with sphinxes. The principal sphinx avenue at Karnak, leading to the entrance in the first pylon, consists of ram-headed sphinxes, creatures with lion bodies and ram heads, the ram being an animal form of the god Amun-Re. Between the front legs of each of these 'criosphinxes' stands a figure of Ramesses II shown as Osiris, in most cases later usurped by Pinodjem, high priest of Amun-Re in the 21st dynasty. In this plate two side views and one front view of two of these sphinxes are shown. An added text of uncertain cryptic sense is carved in Greek letters on the side of the lower sphinx. When the first pylon was added to the great temple of Karnak, probably during the 30th dynasty, this sphinx avenue was cut short and the superfluous sphinxes were stored in close lines in the first court, where they can still be seen. By far the longest avenue of sphinxes led from the south side of Karnak all the way to the Luxor temple. This avenue of traditional sphinxes with royal heads was established by King Nectanebo I of the 30th dynasty, and its best preserved part can be seen at the Luxor end.

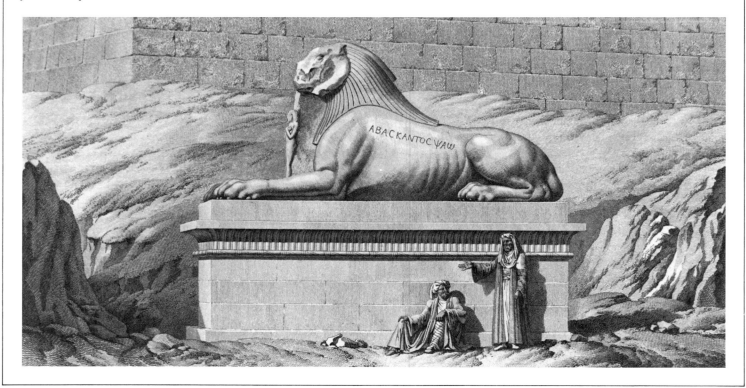

In this imaginative reconstruction, the artists of the Description attempt, with considerable success, to give an impression of the great hypostyle hall in the temple of Amun-Re at Karnak, so called because its distinguishing feature comprises the 134 huge columns which supported the roof. The view presented here looks down the central nave which is flanked by 12 columns topped by capitals in the form of open papyrus flowers. Beyond lies the first court of the temple where a reconstruction of the colonnade of King Taharqa of the 25th dynasty can be seen. The 12 columns of the central nave are 71 feet high, rising 22 feet above the remaining 122 columns in the hall. This extra height allows for the introduction of slatted windows at the top of the nave on both sides, forming a kind of clerestory. The artist has suggested the presence of these windows by the shaft of light slanting down from the left in the foreground. The reliefs and inscriptions in the hypostyle hall are mostly the work of the reigns of Sethos I and Ramesses II of the 19th dynasty. The latter is named and represented on most of the columns, but the decoration shown on the plate only approximately reproduces what was carved.

PLATE 24 TEMPLE SCENES FROM KARNAK AND LUXOR

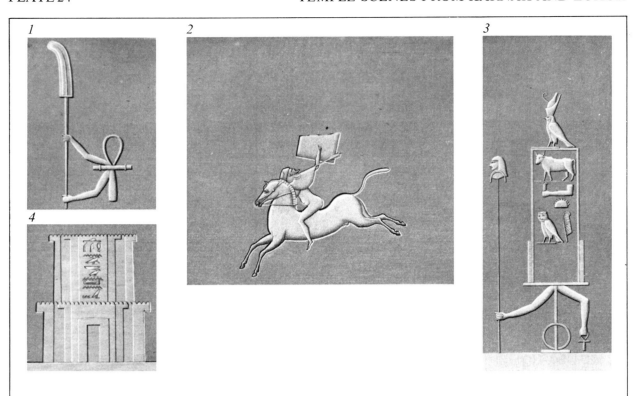

The various scenes reproduced on this plate come mostly from a series of exceptionally fine reliefs carved on the outside of the northern wall of the great hypostyle hall at Karnak. The subject is the campaign conducted in his first regnal year by King Sethos I in Palestine and Syria. The two most interesting are nos. 5 and 6, the first of which shows Sethos, dismounted from his chariot and receiving the submission of the chieftains of the Lebanon. Meanwhile, on the left of the scene are shown the cedar trees of the Lebanon, conventionally represented, some of which are being felled at the request of the king. In the lower of the two scenes Sethos is shown at full charge in his chariot, attacking the Palestinians, many of whom lie slain by his arrows. The Palestinians are defending the fortress of Pakanaan, which is shown on the plate as no. 4. Also belonging to the same scene on the wall is the fan held by arms issuing from an ankh-sign of life, reproduced here as no. 1. The man on horseback in no. 2 comes from another part of the same sequence of reliefs. He is a Syrian and he forms part of an episode in which Sethos is depicted in his chariot attacking Syrians in chariots. No. 3 does not come from the Sethos series, but is extracted from scenes in the Luxor temple depicting the divine birth of King Amenophis III. Here is shown the 'ka' or spirit of the king represented in a formalised manner and incorporating his Horus-name.

The most important and the most secret part of any Egyptian temple was the shrine which contained the image of the temple deity. At Karnak successive shrines of the New Kingdom were replaced by a massive granite sanctuary erected by Philip Arrhidaeus, brother of Alexander the Great, who ruled Egypt for a few years after the death of Alexander and before the establishment of the Ptolemaic dynasty. The plate shows scenes carved on the exterior of this granite shrine. Two registers are reproduced. In the upper a series of episodes in the king's coronation is shown; from the left, the purification of the king by Thoth and Horus, his crowning by Thoth and Horus, his being conducted to Thoth by Atum and Montu, and his kneeling before Amun and Amunet (the female counterpart of Amun). In the lower register are representations of parts of the important Festival of the Valley: boats containing the divine image are shown, two on shrines, and two carried by priests.

This reconstruction shows the east side of the first court which lies immediately within what was, and still is, the principal entrance to the temple of Amun-Re at Karnak. The chief elements which can be seen date from very different periods: the great double pylon – now known as the second pylon – is of the reigns of Horemheb (18th dynasty) and Sethos I (19th dynasty), the colonnade of pillars is of Taharqa (25th dynasty), the small temple on the right is of Ramesses III (20th dynasty), and the low colonnade on the left is of the 22nd dynasty. It is unlikely that the court ever presented an appearance such as is depicted here. The most uncertain part of the reconstruction is the decoration shown on the pylons, which are now very ruined with little decoration visible. Here the artist has drawn freely on the scenes illustrating Ramesses II's victory at Kadesh still to be seen at Luxor (pl. 18). Of the Taharqa pillars one only of the original ten survives. The artist has here shown twelve. In spite of its 'invented' features, this reconstruction yet gives a noble impression of the approach to a great Egyptian temple in its heyday, with tall flagpoles rising high above the façade carrying pennants fluttering in the breeze.

All the sculptures shown on this plate come from the Karnak complex of temples and can be identified with certainty. Nos. 1 and 2 show one of the many seated figures of the goddess Sekhmet which have been found in the temple of Mut, but which probably came originally from the funerary temple of King Amenophis III in western Thebes. This statue, now in the British Museum, is inscribed for Amenophis as 'beloved of Sekhmet, mistress of the goddesses'. No. 3 is the upper part of a colossal Sekhmet still to be found in the temple of Mut, surveying the ruins of the great structure with baleful eye. Nos. 4 and 5 are two views of the granite statue of Roy, a high priest of Amun, also now in the British Museum. A famous official in the reigns of Ramesses II and Sethos II, he is shown seated on the ground with his knees drawn up close to his body, and supporting a divine emblem incorporating the head of the goddess Hathor surmounted by a pylon-shaped element. This emblem represents the sistrum, a percussive instrument used in religious ceremonies. No. 6 is the colossal statue of Ramesses described on pl. 21.

PLATE 28   COLOSSI OF MEMNON

The Colossi of Memnon stand on the west bank of the Nile at Thebes, the modern Luxor. They once fronted the mortuary temple of Amenophis III, only vestiges of which now remain. The two seated sandstone statues represent the king, and the female figure by the right knee of the nearer statue is the great royal wife, Tiye. On the side of the throne are representations of Nile gods tying together the symbolic plants of Upper and Lower Egypt. It was the farther, northern colossus that was associated with Memnon, the Ethiopian hero and son of the Dawn, who fought at Troy and was killed by Achilles. Perhaps as a result of damage in the earthquake of 27 B.C., the statue is said by the Greek geographer Strabo to have emitted a musical sound as the sun rose. This was supposed to be the statue's greeting to his mother, Eos. The musical statue became a considerable tourist attraction. The sound ceased when the upper part of the statue was restored by Septimius Severus in the 3rd century A.D.

Thҍis view of the Ramesseum – the Memnonium or Tomb of Ozymandyas – is almost precisely what is first seen
by modern visitors who enter the great temple enclosure through the gate in the northern wall. On the right are
the best preserved parts of the temple, the entrance to them being marked by the four headless colossal statues of
the god Osiris. These are engaged to square pillars forming part of the colonnade of the second open court of the temple.
Passing up a short flight of steps leading between these statues, the visitor walks into an hypostyle hall with 48 papyrus
columns, and therefore relatively small compared with that at Karnak with its 134 papyrus columns. Behind this hall,
where the roof can be seen to be well preserved, is the so-called Astronomical Room and an Inner Room beyond which is
a small pillared hall and the ruined temple sanctuary. The mass of masonry on the left of the plate represents all that
remains of the eastern side of the second court including part of the colonnade with further colossal Osiris figures, and a
section of the great pylon which formed the eastern wall of the court. On the far left can be seen the tumbled wreck of what
was probably the largest monolithic colossus ever carved in Egypt, a seated granite statue of Ramesses II. When erected
in its glory it stood about 52½ feet tall.

PLATE 30

PLAN AND ELEVATIONS OF THE RAMESSEUM

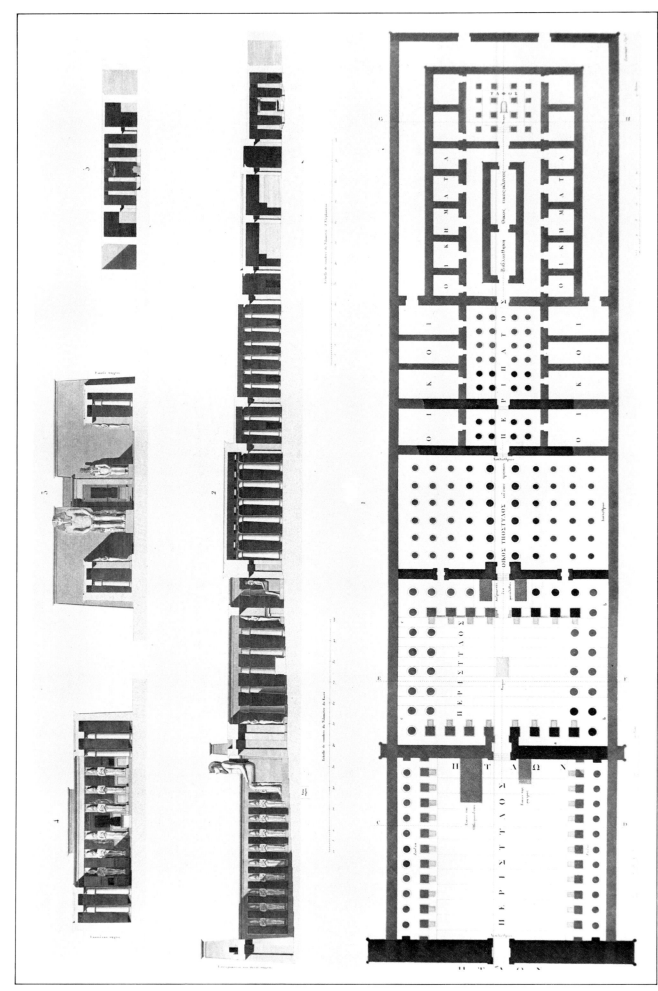

At the time when Napoleon invaded Egypt very little was known about the ancient Egyptians, and scholars were greatly dependent on the accounts of Egypt and its monuments contained in the works of the classical authors like Herodotus, Diodorus Siculus and Plutarch. Diodorus, in discussing the monuments of the Theban area, gives a fairly circumstantial account of a vast building which he describes as the tomb of Ozymandyas. This can easily be identified as the temple now called the Ramesseum, the mortuary chapel for the cult of the dead king Ramesses II. From the remains still visible in the 18th century, the Napoleonic scholars were able to associate many of the more obvious parts of the Ramesseum with elements described and designated by Diodorus. The plan, cross-sections and elevations shown on this plate represent the results of the French interpretation of Diodorus's description. While the great courts and hypostyle hall on the left-hand side of the plan are relatively close to the reality of the remains of the Ramesseum, the parts on the right-hand side are very largely unrelated to the temple as it can be seen today. Two hundred years ago the details of much of the temple layout were hidden beneath huge mounds of debris and unavailable for inspection.

The siege of Dapur is represented in the mortuary temple of Ramesses II known as the Ramesseum, on the west bank at Thebes. The scene appears on the southern entrance wall of the great hypostyle hall. The exact location of Dapur is unknown. It was a Syrian city within the Hittite sphere of influence to the north-west of Kadesh. Ramesses II dates its capture to year 8 of his reign, c. 1271 B.C. The French artist has captured the essence of the scene, with its colourful action. The rocky escarpment on which the fortress is built, its succession of towers and the elaborate nature of its defensive layers are clearly shown. But the scene is much simplified as against the original. It omits part of the fortress, many of the combatants, and the hieroglyphic texts giving the name of the city and identifying the heavily-shielded figures in the lower register as sons of Ramesses. There was apparently no time to draw the lively scene on the left, where the Egyptian chariotry and the king approached the city, some of the inhabitants are already being killed, and the king's son Khaemwaset has his sword at the throat of a Hittite chieftain.

T he best preserved of the royal mortuary temples at Thebes is that built at Medinet Habu for Ramesses III of the 20th dynasty. The huge enclosure surrounding the temple, however, contains much more than this principal structure. Some of the additional buildings are older, and others much younger, than the 20th dynasty. The structures on the left of this plate are part of the main complex of the mortuary temple, and represent the formal gateway which looks much more like a fortress entrance than the door of a great temple enclosure. The fortress character of this High Gate, as it is called, is emphasised on the outside by scenes of the king engaged in the ever popular activity of smiting his enemies. But rooms within the structure have reliefs showing the king at leisure with his ladies. This part of the temple has been called, probably erroneously, the royal harem; but it was surely here where the king might go for a few private relaxations during his formal visits to the temple when it was being built. The small pylon, pillared portico, and walled court extending beyond the limits of the main temple wall, in the centre and to the right of the plate, are Ptolemaic and Roman additions to a small temple dedicated to a special form of the god Amun, which already stood on the site before Ramesses III chose it for his mortuary temple. In the distance can be seen the Ramesseum, the mortuary temple of Ramesses II.

The reconstructed view given in this plate shows part of the inside of the small temple at Deir el-Medina, which lies to the west of the Ramesseum in the Theban hills, at the entrance to the valley occupied by the ancient village in which lived the workmen who constructed the royal tombs at Thebes. At the time when the material for the Description was compiled, the village had not yet been discovered, but the small temple in its enclosure was accessible. Built during the Ptolemaic dynasty, this small temple was dedicated principally to the goddess Hathor, and it may have been built to replace an earlier structure dedicated to the goddess, who was an object of special devotion to the villagers of Deir el-Medina. What is shown in this plate is the diminutive vestibule or pronaos, which stretches across the width of the temple in front of three sanctuaries. The pronaos façade has two central columns with composite papyrus capitals linked by low intercolumnar walls to two square pillars with Hathor heads as capitals. The two central columns carry representations not of gods in the strictest sense, but of two 'real' Egyptian commoners, Imhotep (3rd dynasty) and Amenhotep, son of Hapu (18th dynasty), both of whom attained exceptional fame during their lifetimes, and were subsequently greatly revered as demigods, especially during the Ptolemaic period.

These harpists and their magnificent instruments were first published to the modern world by James Bruce in his Travels to Discover the Source of the Nile *(1790). They occur in the tomb of Ramesses III in the Valley of the Kings. The scenes are in a side room to the left of the descending corridor and are now badly damaged; but harps of this size are represented nowhere else in Egypt. Both are arched harps and both have an elaborately painted soundbox made in two pieces. They are decorated at the lower end with a royal head, the upper wearing the red crown of Lower Egypt, the other wearing a double crown. The upper instrument has 11 strings but should in reality have only 10 fixing pegs. The upper player is described as 'the harpist who makes ready the hall for the gods who are at peace', the lower is 'the harpist who is at the head of the underworld'. The god in the upper scene is Onuris-Shu, son of Re; in the lower Shu, son of Re. The nature of the music being played is unknown, since no notation has come down from ancient Egypt.*

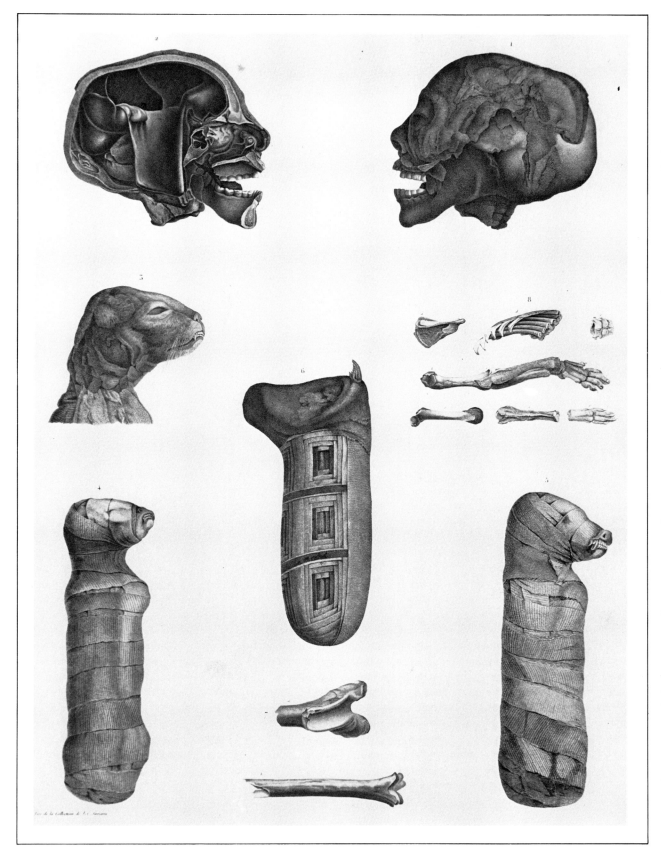

In most people's minds the ancient Egyptians are closely associated with death and burial, chiefly because the physical trappings of death and burial have been preserved in such quantities from ancient Egypt. The tombs in the Theban necropolis provided almost ideal conditions for the preservation of all kinds of materials which commonly perish in the damp graves of other ancient cultures, and even in other parts of ancient Egypt. Travellers to Egypt from the early 19th century onwards were fascinated by mummies, and enterprising villagers who lived among the tombs of Thebes were adept at finding mummies to offer to wealthy tourists. Almost better than a mummy was a mummy's head, especially if it retained its skin and presented some life-like appearance. A head such as that shown on this plate could very conveniently be carried in a hat-box, and was a fine reminder of mortality as well as being a splendid trophy to take home. This plate also carries drawings of mummified cats and a dog (centre), as well as miscellaneous bones from other mummified fauna. In the last centuries of the pharaonic period and in Graeco-Roman times, the practice of mummifying the animals sacred to certain cults became widespread and animal cemeteries were established in many parts of Egypt. Such animal mummies, often wrapped with elaborate care in linen bandages, were offered as votive presentations by pious visitors to the appropriate shrines.

PLATE 36

TEMPLE OF DENDERA

The façade of the Ptolemaic temple of Dendera is here disfigured by the ruins of brick houses on the roof, and there is still much sand on the north-eastern side of the building. Frenchmen are shown at work recording the temple, and their tent is to the right. A Greek inscription, not copied for the plate, dates the dedication of the building to the reign of Tiberius. On the façade are cartouches of Tiberius, Caligula and Claudius; they worship Hathor of Dendera, the goddess of the temple, here consort of Horus of Edfu, and the child gods Harsomtus (Horus, uniter of the Two Lands) and Ihy, patron of music. The artist has clearly delineated the 24 columns of the outer hypostyle hall. The exterior side walls of the temple have scenes connected with the construction and dedication of the building. The emperor Augustus is shown leaving the royal palace, measuring the ground plan for the future temple, offering bricks to the deities of Dendera, laying a stone block with the help of Hathor, and finally presenting the completed building to Hathor and Horus.

PLATE 37

REAR WALL AT DENDERA

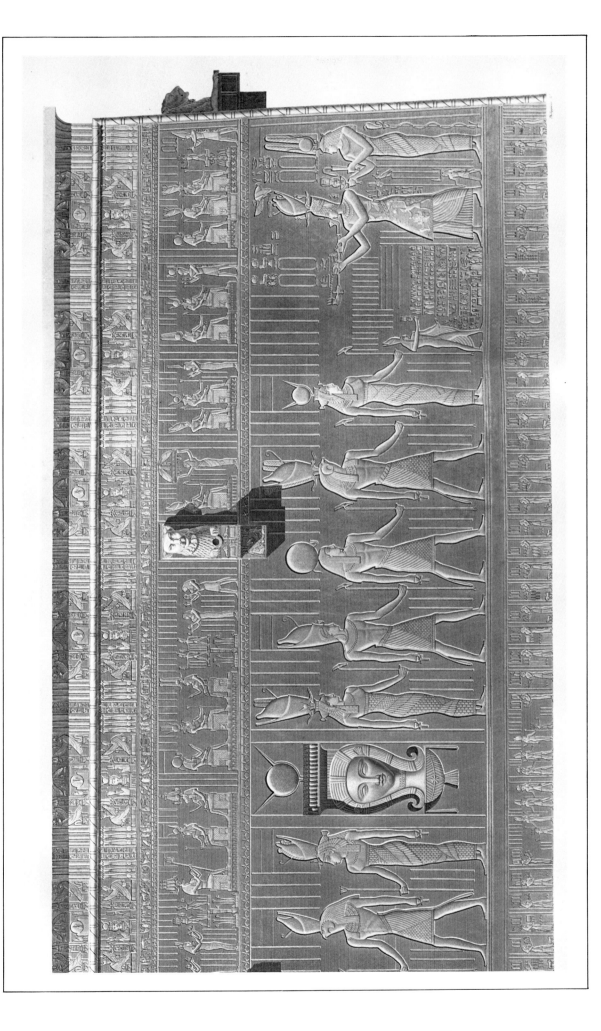

T he rear exterior wall of the Dendera temple has as its centre an image of the goddess Hathor, which faces south towards the temple of her consort, Horus of Edfu. On the same level as the lion-headed gargoyle, at once guardian and waterspout, the two right hand scenes show Augustus offering a figure of Maat, goddess of truth, and a pair of mirrors to various deities; immediately right of the gargoyle a goddess holds up the heavens before Horus. The large scene depicts Caesarion burning incense; behind him is his mother Cleopatra the Great holding cult objects associated with Hathor. They stand before the gods most worshipped at Dendera: a small Ihy, then Hathor, Horus of Edfu, Harsomtus, a full-sized Ihy and Hathor again. This is now the sole surviving representation of Cleopatra and Caesarion. The main features of the frieze, which was decorated by Augustus, are the repeated reliefs of the sun rising over the horizon with Hathor heads below. The base of the wall shows figures of the different Egyptian districts approaching the gods of Dendera. Because of the time spent in clearing the lower part of the scene, the French artists were prevented from copying all the hieroglyphs.

PLATE 38   HYPOSTYLE HALL AT DENDERA

This artistic impression of the outer hypostyle hall at Dendera shows a procession in honour of the goddess Isis rather than the more appropriate Hathor. The original commentary on the plate emphasises that considerable sand clearance was needed before the column bases could be reached and the exact height of the hall established. The astronomical ceiling dates to the reign of Tiberius. There are zodiacs, hymns to Isis and the dog-star, 12 boats of the sun-god Re representing the hours of the day, 12 representing the night, and the phases of the moon. The texts on the south wall to the right are shared mainly between Augustus and Caligula. The former is shown presenting an obelisk to the gods; Caligula follows a bull-headed deity into the presence of Harsomtus and Hathor. But in most of the scenes in the hall the protagonist is Nero. He leaves the royal palace in company of his double for purification with the waters of life by Horus and Thoth; he is crowned by Buto, serpent goddess of the north, and Nekhbet, the vulture of the south; and he makes a variety of offerings to countless gods.

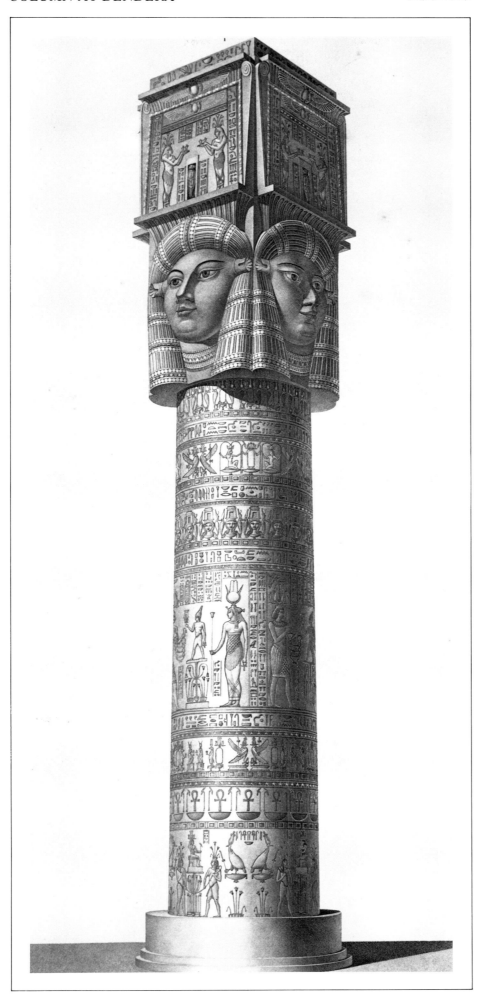

The 24 columns of the outer hypostyle hall at Dendera carry cartouches of Claudius. At the foot of the column are Nile gods uniting the Two Lands. The large central scene has Claudius to the right; to the left is Hathor, and in front of her the child-god Ihy holding a sistrum in the shape of a naos or shrine. The elements of this sistrum, the favourite instrument of the cow-goddess Hathor, are similar to those of the column itself. The sistrum handle is equivalent to the column shaft; there is a Hathor head with cow's ears and straight-ended wig above; and on top is a model shrine (the column here shows the side volutes which represent stylised cow's horns), through which, in the case of the musical instrument, pass the sounding rods of what is essentially a kind of rattle. The hieroglyphs on the column have been arranged haphazardly. In the first edition of the Description this plate was coloured, since at the time of the expedition there were distinct traces of original colour in the hall.

PLATE 40

SCENES FROM DENDERA

Of these five scenes in the temple of Dendera only nos. 1 and 2 survive. Scene 1 is on the east exterior wall of the main temple and could be readily copied only because the level of the surrounding sand was so high. It is in the top register and shows the king offering to the ithyphallic god Min; between them is the mast of Min; the mast is supported by four ropes and against it are four poles up which pairs of Nubians are climbing, probably in a race to the top. Scene 2 is from the western wing of the propylon to the temple, decorated mainly by Domitian; lion-headed genii with knives appear on nine registers in all. Scenes 3-5 are from the pylon of a temple dedicated probably to Harsomtus, which was in the town enclosure east of the main temple; it no longer exists. The cartouches on the pylon carried the names of Tiberius, Antoninus Pius and Marcus Aurelius. In the three scenes the emperor is engaged in acts of slaughter before Horus and Hathor. In scene 3 he slays Asiatics with the assistance of a lion; in scene 4 he kills a hippopotamus; and in scene 5 the victim is a crocodile. Both these animals were associated with the god Seth, main enemy of Horus.

Of the two birth houses at Dendera, the later one provided the materials for this plate. It was built by Augustus and decorated mainly by Trajan and Hadrian. The purpose of the building was to celebrate the divine birth of the child-gods Ihy and Harsomtus and at the same time that of pharaoh himself. A colonnade surrounds the temple, and part of the cornice is represented in scene 1. Beneath a winged scarab is a figure of Horus; on either side Trajan offers a sistrum to Isis, and a figure of Maat stands behind a monumental cartouche. Scene 2 is from the inner face of the colonnade, showing a section of the architrave and the abaci of two columns. At the centre a figure of the child-god Ihy emerges from a lotus, observed on either side by Bes and Thoeris, both associated with child-birth; the outstretched wings of a falcon protect the cartouches of Antoninus Pius. On the abacus of each column is a figure of Bes holding a bouquet. The Bes heads of the frieze rest on the sign for gold and each has a naos above with a uraeus on either side (not the gazelle head suggested by the plate).

PLATE 42   TEMPLE OF ANTAEOPOLIS

The temple of Antaeopolis stood on the east bank of the Nile, some 25 miles south of Asyut. The course of the river was at that time further east than now, and the temple ruins were gradually undermined by the Nile. The building was Ptolemaic, and the cartouche of Ptolemy IV was recorded there. The 18 columns of the hypostyle hall were still standing in 1813. The palm-leaf capitals were the more impressive for the thick row of palm trees that formed their background. Blocks from the entablature are scattered in the foreground; most of them had hieroglyphic inscriptions, but the central ones were carved in Greek. By 1817 most of the columns were lying on their side by the river, with only one left standing. Two years later the whole of the building had collapsed as a result of an unusually high inundation; and in 1821 the greater part of the temple was swept away by the Nile. This was one year before Champollion published his initial letter on the decipherment of hieroglyphics; and so the details of the temple texts can never be known.

The name Antaeopolis was connected by the Greeks with the Libyan giant Antaeus, who was killed by Herakles. It was not only his name that had similarities with the local god Antywey; this god seems to have been both a form of Horus and also equated with Seth. Diodorus preserves the tradition that the battle between Horus and Seth took place near the village of Antaeus. Parts of the Greek inscription on the entablature of the portico are visible on the plate; it was this inscription which proved the identity of the ancient Antaeopolis with the village of Qaw el-Kebir, part of which appears to the left. The inscription was set up by Ptolemy VI and his wife Cleopatra; an addition to it reveals that the Roman emperors Marcus Aurelius and Lucius Verus undertook some restoration in the temple. Local inhabitants can be seen to the right, and to the left are French experts preparing to plan and record the temple. The original commentary on the plate draws attention to the forked date palm in front of the village; the expedition saw none other like it.

PLATE 44

TEMPLE OF ANTAEOPOLIS

The conjectural restoration of the temple of Antaeopolis has kept the Nile at a safe distance. Instead of the Greek inscription above the entrance, the artist has restored the original winged disc, symbolic of Horus's victory over the enemies of the sungod. The back part of the temple has been renewed and the complex given a brick enclosure wall. Fragments of the stone wall to the right were in existence at the time of the expedition; two Egyptian priests have been resurrected to give an idea of its scale. One of the most remarkable relics of the site was a monolithic pyramidal naos that lay behind the temple and directly on its axis. A frieze of scarabs decorated the inside of the shrine, and the original commentary praised the fineness of its hieroglyphs while lamenting there was no time to copy them. It may be assumed that the artist has restored the naos to the temple sanctuary and installed in it a statue of Antewey, the local god. The absence of screen walls on the façade has given Ptolemaic Egypt a new architectural motif, at once attractive and highly conjectural.

The western mountains behind Asyut, the ancient Lycopolis, have a number of important tombs, mainly of the 12th dynasty. The mountain was also used by early Christian hermits, and quarrying took place there. The local god was Wepwawet, 'opener of the ways', probably in origin a wild dog. The Middle Kingdom citizens of Asyut gave the first fruits of each harvest to the local temple in his honour. The Greeks equated the god with a wolf; hence their name Lycopolis for the city. The road leading to the mountains was raised on a dyke, as the inundation flooded the plain on either side. The houses bordering it belonged to Mamelukes. The nearest one was taken over by the French as their headquarters. The roof has been crenellated and a cannon mounted on top. About to march out of the western gate of the town is a detachment of French troops returning from an operation against the Mamelukes. A cannon is being dragged at the front, a camel loaded with standards follows behind. In the foreground is a local inhabitant appalled that his wife should approach within sight of the French.

PLATE 46   SCENES FROM ASYUT TOMB

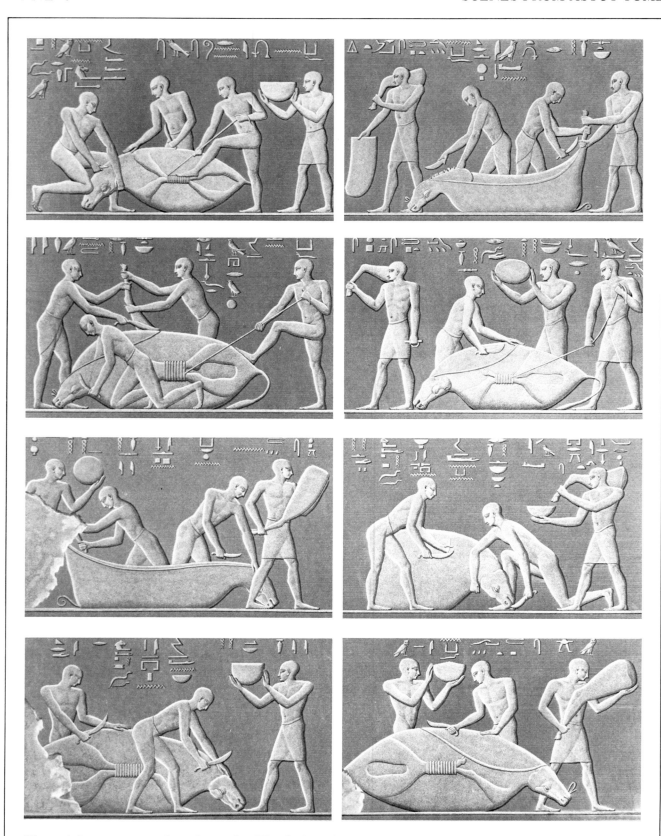

These eight scenes come from the tomb of Hepdjefa in the western mountains at Asyut. He was governor of the Lycopolite district, chancellor of the king of Lower Egypt, and overseer of the local priests. He held office under Sesostris I of the 12th dynasty; a statue of Hepdjefa and his wife has been found in a tomb at the ancient Egyptian trading centre of Kerma, south of the Third Cataract in the Sudan. On the strength of the statue it has been suggested that he was a Viceroy of Kush who died at his post. The Asyut tomb is unfinished. The most important inscription in the tomb is concerned with ten contracts to ensure for Hepdjefa that certain ceremonies would be performed and offerings made by the priests of Asyut. In the sixth contract Hepdjefa as governor makes a contract with himself as overseer of priests. The scenes of making oxen ready for sacrifice appeared on both sides of the innermost shrine; they have since been destroyed.

This tomb, already ruinous on its northern side, no longer exists. It belonged to a local governor of Asyut called Hepdjefa, a man with similar titles to those of his namesake on the previous plate and probably of the same family. These rulers owed their political power to the kings of the 12th dynasty, who well understood the strategic importance of Asyut. Other tombs in the mountains record how in a previous generation the local princes had supported the weak royal house based at Heracleopolis and had held at bay the Theban upstarts who were eventually to found the 11th dynasty. Hepdjefa is represented to the left of the entrance with mace and staff of office. He was an overseer of prophets of Osiris and Wepwawet, two gods closely associated in the solemn mystery plays at Abydos. It was Wepwawet, god of Asyut, who sought out the enemies of Osiris and avenged his death. A rough passage to the right used to lead to the tomb of the other Hepdjefa. French artists are shown busy at their work, with two locals in attendance.

PLATE 48   PORTICO AT HERMOPOLIS

Nothing now remains of the temple built by Alexander the Great and Philip Arrhidaeus at Hermopolis Magna. The modern name of the site is Ashmunein, which still enshrines the Egyptian word for the eight primeval gods of the place. The Greeks named the city Hermopolis because of the supposed similarity between their Hermes and the Egyptian god of wisdom, Thoth. The façade of the portico had a frieze decorated with cartouches of Alexander the Great, which were carved also on the soffits of the columns; the same king was shown before a variety of gods on the architraves. On the inner face of the architraves were a dedication text of Philip Arrhidaeus, Alexander's shadowy successor, and scenes in which he made offering to Thoth. The papyrus bud capitals of the 12 columns are similar to those of the open court at Luxor built by Amenophis III. The original commentary describes the monument as one of the most splendid to survive from ancient Egypt, on which there were still traces of brilliant colour. The temple was built of limestone, and the absence of fallen blocks in the area gave rise to the theory that the local inhabitants had burnt them for fertiliser. The portico was destroyed in 1822.

PLATE 49

ANTINOOPOLIS

A ntinoopolis was founded by the emperor Hadrian in A.D. 130. It was built to commemorate the drowning of his favourite Antinous in the Nile nearby. Little of the city now remains. The initial inhabitants were of Greek origin, and the plan of the city was typically Hellenistic, with the main streets crossing at right angles. The city grew in importance, and during the Byzantine period was the capital of the Thebaid. The hippodrome in the desert area to the east can be seen in the right background of the view above. The main line of columns there marks the street that led from the triumphal arch by the Nile to the eastern gate, of which the two lofty Corinthian columns appear to stretch half way up the mountains. The group of columns inside and to the right of the gate belonged to the public baths. The columns in the right foreground led to the gateway of the theatre along another main street. The mounds that cover much of the scene had grown up over the ancient ruins. Extensive quarries for the area are in the eastern mountains behind. A camel caravan can be seen approaching from the north.

PLATE 50   THEATRE GATEWAY AT ANTINOOPOLIS

The gateway of the theatre at Antinoopolis marked the formal southern end of one of the city's main streets running parallel to the Nile. It was the lofty columns of this gateway, with their finely carved Corinthian capitals, that indicated the site of Antinoopolis above the date palms bordering the river. The upper part of the gateway was already destroyed at the time of the expedition, and nothing remained of the entablature or the pediment. Numerous lime kilns in the area told their sad story of steady destruction. Tradition has it that the wooden gates, plated with iron, were later taken to Cairo and hung at the great gate of Bab Zuwaila. It seems that beyond the gate was a large square with an Ionic colonnade. This led in turn to the amphitheatre, of which only extensive ruins remained when the French were there. The proscenium could be made out, marked by six pillars. French artists are at work on the left; French soldiers are posted by the column to the right; and a group of locals eyes the whole operation.

The plate shows elevations, sections and details of the gateway of the theatre at Antinoopolis. The elevation of scene 2 has restored the top of the central doorway and added eight courses of stone to reach the level of the column capitals. In scene 1 six steps have been added so as to accommodate the base of the columns and the threshold of the doorway; an entablature and pediment have been suggested above. Scenes 3 - 7 are concerned with details of the columns, their bases and capitals, shown in section and in profile. Scene 8 gives enlarged details of one of the windows in the gateway. Since there was already uncertainty about the lateral extent of the gateway, no attempt was made to reconstruct the sides.

PLATE 52   TRIUMPHAL ARCH AT ANTINOOPOLIS

The triumphal arch at Antinoopolis was the best preserved of the Roman monuments at the time of the expedition. The granite columns that stood in front of the Corinthian pilasters and originally supported colossal statues were already missing; though their much damaged bases were still in position. The columns had probably been removed to some church or mosque. Four circular staircases led to the top of the monument. Between the triumphal arch and the river was a vast square surrounded by red granite columns, of which the French found seven still in place. These columns had Corinthian capitals in limestone, which suggested the columns themselves might once have been used elsewhere, perhaps at Hermopolis on the other side of the Nile. Two vast pedestals beyond the arch in the direction of the river were undoubtedly statue bases. The French artist has shown the village of Sheikh Abadeh on the further side of the arch. A number of Frenchmen are planning the different parts of the monument and are watched by local inhabitants. There appeared to be no inscription on the monument, which would accord with Hadrian's habitual reluctance to impress his own name on the architecture of the empire.

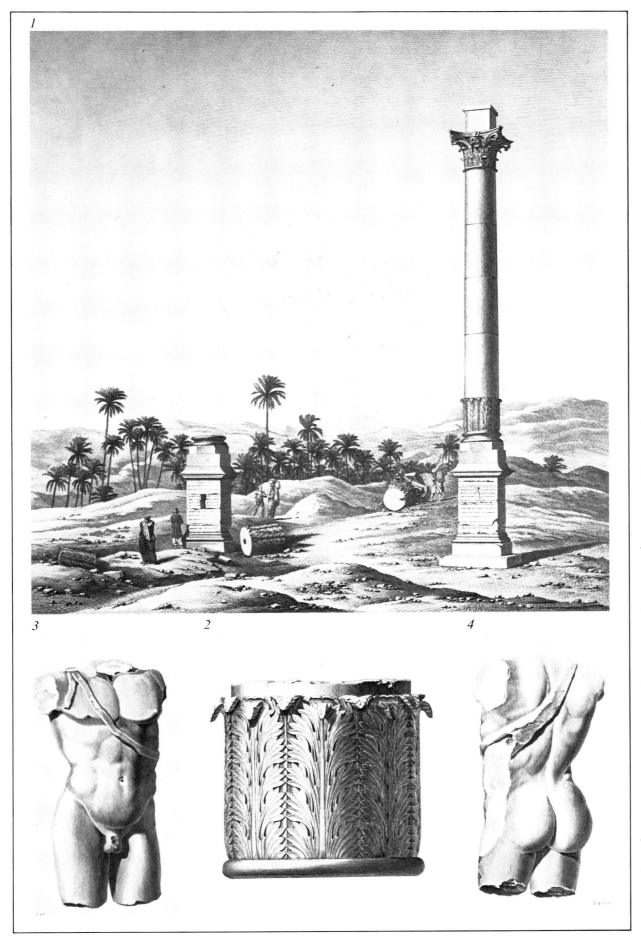

One of the main street intersections at Antinoopolis was decorated with columns set up in honour of the emperor Alexander Severus. This particular intersection lay in the north part of the city. It seems certain that the columns originally carried statues. When the French visited, two of the columns had already fallen nearby; of the third only the base and a portion of the drum remained; the fourth was intact, except for the statue. The shape of the pedestal is unusual, and the column rests on an octagonal support. A Greek inscription of 14 lines on the two pedestals records the dedication to Alexander Severus and his mother Julia Mamaea. The olive-leaf decoration at the foot of the column struck the French as worthy of special comment, and a detail of it appears on the plate. The columns may have been set up to celebrate the inconclusive Persian campaign of Alexander against the Sassanid Ardashir that ended in A.D. 233. Scenes 3 and 4 represent a life-size statue of Antinous found near the triumphal arch. Only the torso was recovered despite diligent search for the rest of the body. The statue was taken to Cairo but subsequently lost. The Antinous type, youthful but of a certain languor, is well represented by the fragment.

PLATE 54   STABLES OF ANTAR AND BENI HASAN SCENES

Scene 1 depicts an impressive outcrop of rock; its remarkable shape has been caused by extensive quarrying. The inside has been quarried too, so that the whole resembles a mighty building with many entrances. Known locally as the Stables of Antar (a mythical giant), it provided a refuge for farmers and their animals at the time of the inundation. It lies south of Beni Hasan, whence the other scenes come. The rock tombs of Beni Hasan, high and imposing in the eastern cliffs, commemorate a line of local governors belonging to the Oryx nome, the 16th district of Upper Egypt. These scenes are all from tomb no. 2, which belongs to Amenemhat, an official under Sesostris I of the 12th dynasty. Scenes 2a and 2b come from the west wall of the main hall. The harvesting and ploughing appear in the tomb as shown, though the three men preparing flax to the right of scene 2b should properly be in a register above. Scene 4 from the east wall is a funerary boat carrying a mummy, and scene 3 may be a free interpretation of a boat engaged in the pilgrimage to Abydos on the same wall.

These scenes come from five different tombs of the 11th and 12th dynasties at Beni Hasan, though not all of them can be readily identified. The first two scenes are characteristic work of the Beni Hasan artists. Wrestling, with other forms of physical and military training, appear frequently among the scenes, a reminder that the transition from the First Intermediate Period had not been easy. Scene 1 is in fact from two different tombs, no. 2 (Amenemhat) and no. 15 (Bakt); scene 2 is from tomb no. 17 (Kheti). Other common representations at Beni Hasan are the care of domestic animals and hunting in the desert. Scene 3 is from tomb no. 3 (Khnumhotep), and scene 4, with its realistic terrain and manifest terror of the gazelles, from the tomb of Amenemhat. Scenes 5-7 are concerned with offerings for the deceased, the first two from the tomb of Kheti, the third from tomb no. 23 (Neterkhet). There are many musical scenes at Beni Hasan, with the harp often featured, either in the hands of a man or a woman. Scene 9 shows a female player, who sits immediately behind a male harpist in the actual tomb. The man being beaten in scene 10 is in the tomb of Bakt, and he seems to have been a defaulter at a stock-taking of oxen.

PLATE 56 TEMPLE OF QASR QARUN

The late Ptolemaic temple of Qasr Qarun is on the ancient site of Dionysias in the Fayum. It stands at the west end of the Birket Qarun, which is the modern remnant of the Lake Moeris described by Herodotus. The temple is dedicated to Sobek-Re, a conflation of the crocodile-god with the sun-god. The upper scene shows the solid mass of the temple approached by a French detachment to the right, while members of a local tribe lurk behind the sand dunes to the left. The lower view of the temple is taken from the east by moonlight. Some travellers and guides are entering the temple; their encampment is to the right. The forecourt of the temple is ruined, and the damage to the upper part of the pylon allows a view to a second storey, which is an unusual feature in an Egyptian temple. There are 14 subsidiary rooms round the sanctuary, which is divided into three chapels. In one of the upper rooms the king is shown worshipping Sobek in human form. There is a remarkable absence of hieroglyphs throughout the building, both inside and out.

View of pyramids of the Old and Middle Kingdoms in the area of the Fayum and Dahshur. Scene 1 is the brick pyramid of Amenemmes III (12th dynasty) at Hawara. Scene 2 is the brick pyramid of Sesostris II (12th dynasty) at El-Lahun. No. 3 is the Meidum pyramid of Snefru (4th dynasty), one of three gigantic pyramids built by that king. Part of the vast accumulation of debris at the base of the pyramid, familiar to all visitors to the site, has been removed in recent excavations. In nos. 4, 5, and 6 the main monument seen is the so-called 'Bent Pyramid' of Snefru at Dahshur. In no. 6 the broken outline of the mud-brick pyramid of Amenemmes III can be discerned towards the right, and in the far distance the great north or stone pyramid of Snefru, both at Dahshur. In all cases the artist appears to have 'romanticised' the background landscape to some extent, since the desert is not as hilly as the drawings would suggest.

PLATE 58   MAP FROM CAIRO TO MEMPHIS

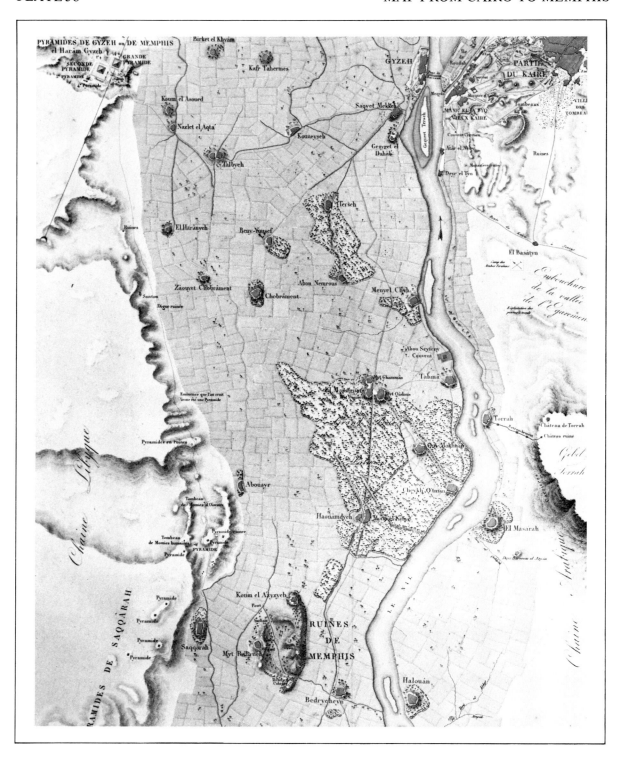

The map shows an extent of the Nile from the island of Roda in the north to beyond Helwan southwards. The Tura Hills, from which came the finest limestone in ancient Egypt, are halfway down on the extreme right. The desert pyramids to the west include those of Giza, Abusir, Saqqara and Dahshur. Centrally placed towards the south are the ruins of Memphis. The French commentary makes the point that the remains of no temple or palace could any longer be seen at Memphis, and no monument remained standing. It would have taken extensive excavation to get any impression of the city said to have stretched a half day's journey in all directions as late as the 12th century A.D. But it was the French achievement to have located Memphis with certainty. So many hieroglyphic blocks had been discovered amid the mounds of rubbish at Mitrahina that there could be no doubt about the identity of the place. Furthermore the site was consistent with information from earlier travellers and geographers. This was indeed the ancient city founded by Menes, first king of the 1st dynasty, the administrative capital of the Two Lands throughout much of Egypt's history, and a teeming cosmopolitan centre of early civilisation.

T hrough a clearing in the palm groves of Memphis can be seen afar the three pyramids of Giza. The flood water, the reeds and the abundance of trees give an impression of why archaeological work at Memphis has always been difficult. The water table is high, the ground has been much farmed and is now much built on. In the foreground of the plate a French engineer oversees the transport of the left hand of a colossal statue. This red granite fragment was discovered at the same time as other parts of the statue by members of the expedition. This find suggests the description by Herodotus of the huge statues set up by Sesostris at the temple of Hephaestus, the Greek name for the local craftsman-god Ptah. The hand was removed to Cairo and Alexandria, where it was reluctantly handed over to the eventual victors and began its journey to the British Museum. Memphis is now particularly associated with the massive limestone statue of Ramesses II, still at the site, and a fine red granite statue of the same pharaoh, now in the main station square of Cairo.

PLATE 60

P anorama of the plateau of Giza seen from the north at sunrise. To the left is the Great Pyramid, the upper 12 courses and the capstone of which were anciently removed for reuse. Adjacent is seen the pyramid of Chephren, the upper courses of the Tura limestone casing of which remain intact. On the far right the third pyramid (of Mycerinus or Menkaure) can be glimpsed. The elevated position occupied by the three famous Giza pyramids is clearly to be seen in this drawing. Later pyramid builders were obliged to move further south for lack of space, and to utilise low-lying stretches of the desert for the most part, though almost without exception the Old Kingdom pyramid complexes were within sight of the ancient capital Memphis.

View of the entrance of the Great Pyramid of Cheops at Giza. Situated in the north face of the monument, about 55 feet above ground level, the entrance gives access to a descending corridor penetrating ultimately deep into the bedrock below the superstructure of the pyramid. The casing blocks of the pyramid had long since been stripped away when this drawing was made, revealing the core blocks of limestone, on average weighing some two and a half tons, cut from local quarries. The immense monoliths over the corridor, and the relieving blocks of the 'arch' above, each about 12 feet long, can be seen in this careful drawing. Somewhat below the original entrance there is another opening roughly cut in the core masonry, though not seen in the illustration. Allegedly this aperture was made on the orders of the caliph Ma'mun, son of Harun el-Rashid (of Arabian Nights fame), searching for hidden treasure. This event took place in the 9th century A.D.

PLATE 62   GRAND GALLERY IN THE GREAT PYRAMID

Perspective views of the interior of the Grand Gallery or ascending corridor of the pyramid of Cheops at Giza. In the drawing to the left members of the expedition are seen investigating a hitherto unexplored chamber at ceiling level. The long portable ladder was made by the architect Le Père, who is seen below gazing up at his intrepid colleague Coulette, assisted by a local, disappearing into the chamber. The view was taken looking towards the north, i.e. towards the entrance to the pyramid. In the scene to the right other French travellers are making their way up the Grand Gallery towards the royal sarcophagus chamber. The mode of construction of the magnificent Gallery, 153 feet long and 28 feet high, with its corbel vault, can be seen in these admirable illustrations.

The plateau at Giza, seen before excavation, with the pyramid of Chephren in the centre. The partly-buried mortuary temple of the king can be observed abutting the east face. To the right lies the Great Pyramid of Cheops, only the south-east corner of which was included by the artist, and in the far distance the funerary monument of Mycerinus with one of its subsidiary or satellite pyramids. In the foreground the trackways crossing the plateau are clearly seen. These have now been obliterated by subsequent archaeological work in the necropolis, which has brought to light streets of mastaba tombs of members of the royal family and high officials of the Old Kingdom.

PLATE 64   GIZA PYRAMIDS AND SPHINX

Geneneral view of the pyramids and Sphinx of Giza, the latter lying near the Valley Temple of the second pyramid (of Chephren, or Khafre, glimpsed to the left). In the background is the Great Pyramid of Cheops (Khufu) and its satellite pyramids. The view was taken at sunset. The Sphinx, the head of which may have been an attempt at a 'portrait' of Chephren, is not, as is sometimes supposed, a colossus made up of separate blocks of stone, but rather is carved from a knoll of living rock left standing by the masons of the pyramid of Cheops when they were quarrying blocks in the vicinity for its inner core. The men seen on the head of the Sphinx give a good idea of its gigantic proportions, its length being about 240 feet and the width of its face over 13 feet. Much of the colossal figure was still masked by windblown sand when the drawing was made. The first modern clearance took place in 1818, and was conducted by Captain Giovanni Battista Caviglia at a cost of £450, a not inconsiderable sum for those days.

The head of the Sphinx, with the Great Pyramid and its satellite pyramids serving as a background. When the drawing was made the Sphinx was still buried up to its shoulders in sand, subsequently cleared by Captain Caviglia. A chapel between the paws of the gigantic beast contained, among other elements, a large but damaged stela commemorating a dream of Tuthmosis IV (18th dynasty) when a prince. We read that when out hunting on the Giza plateau he rested at midday in the shadow of the Sphinx, and while he slept, doubtless against its north or east side, the Sphinx (regarded at this time as an embodiment of the sun-god Harmachis) revealed that if he cleared his body from the superincumbent sand he (Tuthmosis) would receive the double crown and become king. Since Napoleon's expedition the great monument has deteriorated drastically, and urgent restoration work has been put in hand by the Egyptian Antiquities Organisation.

Scenes from two mastaba tombs situated east of the pyramid of Chephren at Giza. Scene 1 shows attendants carrying sacks and other objects; scene 2, men pressing wine; no. 3, attendant holding collars, and a box with collars; no. 4, three bulls; no. 5, a raft with decoy bird at one end; no. 6, men overthrowing a bull prior to slaughter; no. 7, workmen carrying bundles of papyrus and building a papyrus canoe; no. 8, names of funerary estates from which the mortuary priests of the tomb-owner drew their produce for the funerary cult; no. 9, herdsmen leading animals. All these scenes are from the tomb of Nebemakhet, king's son of his body, chief justice and vizier (4th dynasty). Scene 10, two men with an ibex and an oryx, and men carrying a hyena and a goose, is from the tomb of Debhen, overlord of Nekhen, secretary of the toilet house, etc. (4th dynasty, time of Mycerinus). Such scenes provide a fundamental source material for the study of daily life, agricultural activities, and economic history of the Old Kingdom.

PLATE 67

FORTRESS OF BABYLON

T he Roman fortress of Babylon in Old Cairo is now part of the Coptic quarter, with churches built above it and in close proximity. The origins of the fortress are obscure. Its history may have begun during either the Assyrian or Persian occupations of Egypt. It became the headquarters of a Roman legion and extensive rebuilding took place about the time of Trajan. The excellence of the Roman work formed the basis for later additions using poorer materials and less careful building methods. At the time of the French expedition the three great towers of the monument, now reduced to two, were very impressive despite the massive accumulation of rubbish round them. A French architect is planning the building, and at the time the details of the vaulted gateway were much admired. Above the semi-circle of the lower arch a reused hieroglyphic block was observed; on it was the winged disk of ancient Egypt, and its presence was a telling symbol of the march of time. Part of the fortification was dismantled during British rule, but the remainder has been completely excavated.

PLATE 68   OBELISK OF THOTH

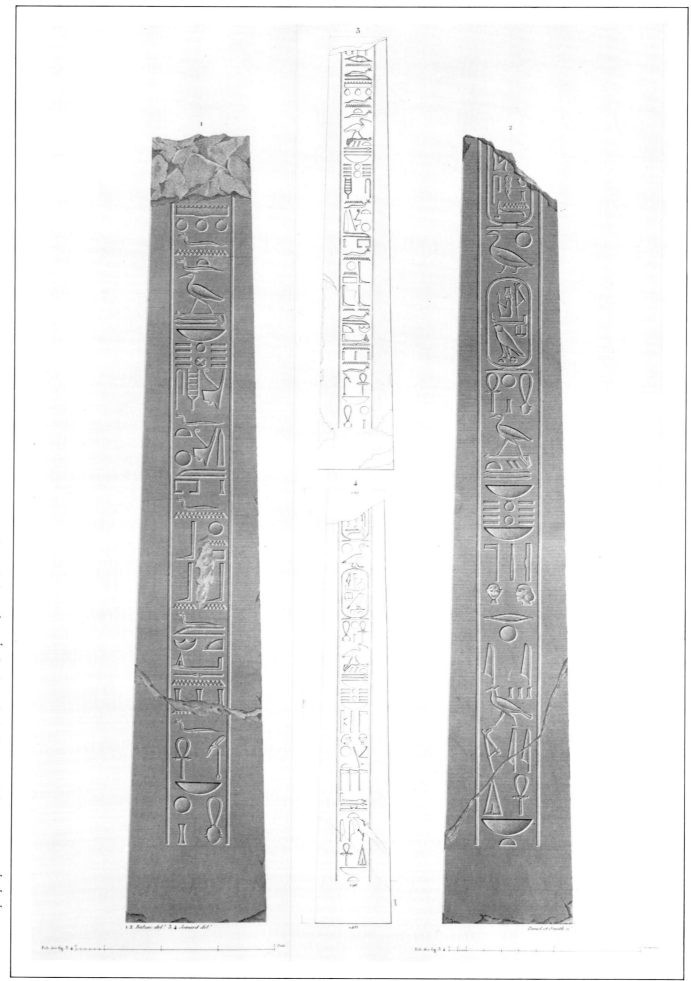

This obelisk is one of a pair now in the sculpture gallery of the British Museum. They seem originally to have been erected before a temple of Thoth in one of the Delta cities, perhaps Hermopolis Parva near modern Aga. The French expedition found the obelisks in front of a Cairo mosque, though they had been seen by Niebuhr in the early 1760s serving as threshold for a mosque in the Citadel. They were taken to Alexandria for shipment to France, but were handed to the British when the capitulation was signed. The hieroglyphs have been mostly well copied, though the grouping is sometimes clumsy and there are some errors. The cartouches are those of Nectanebo II, last king of the 30th dynasty. The inscriptions refer to the setting up of the obelisk in a country seat of Thoth, lord of Ashmunein, lord of the divine word. The obelisk is of fine black basalt and the carving of the highest quality. Its pyramidion was already missing when the French found the monuments.

W hen the French were in Alexandria, one of 'Cleopatra's Needles' was still standing near the shore of the Great Harbour, it is now in Central Park, New York. Another lies hidden in the sand before it; this is on the northern bank of the Thames in London. Both were originally set up by Tuthmosis III in Heliopolis to honour the sun-god Re-Horakhti and celebrate his own third jubilee. Subsidiary inscriptions by Ramesses II and Siamun were added later. Augustus had them removed to Alexandria. In 22 B.C. they were erected in front of the Caesarion, a monument to the deified Julius Caesar intended at first as a tribute by Cleopatra to Mark Antony. The removal of the fallen obelisk to London was planned soon after the defeat of the French in 1801; it was not finally accomplished till 1878. Two years later the standing obelisk was in New York. Both obelisks are here shown against the background of the so-called tower of the Romans. The French savants decided it was indeed Roman because its style differed so markedly from the nearby Arab fortifications. The Pharillon, modest successor to the Pharos lighthouse of old, appears on the Silsila rocks to the left.

PLATE 70   COLUMNS AND MOSQUE AT ALEXANDRIA

The foreground of this scene shows three Graeco-Roman columns such as formed the essential building materials of ancient Alexandria. The mosque behind, which no longer exists in this form, was built on the site of the church of St. Theonas. It was here that Athanasius, whose views had prevailed against those of Arius at the Council of Nicaea in A.D. 325, was surrounded by 5000 Romans on the order of the emperor Constantius 30 years later. Athanasius wisely went into exile; but the mosque retained the association with his name. The most remarkable feature of the mosque for the French was a massive sarcophagus. Covered with inscriptions from the 'Book of What is in the Underworld', it was thought at one time to have housed the burial of Alexander the Great. In fact it is the sarcophagus of Nectanebo II. Twelve holes were drilled in it near the bottom, and for many years it was used as a bath. It is now in the British Museum sculpture gallery, a spoil of the French capitulation.

The monument known as 'Pompey's Pillar' stands to the south-west of modern Alexandria. It was in fact raised by the prefect Postumus to honour in A.D. 300 the emperor Diocletian, who had campaigned in Egypt three years previously against the usurper Achilleus. It may originally have supported an equestrian statue of the emperor. The red granite column possibly came from the temple of Serapis, known to have been nearby on the same hill. The pedestal contains a Greek inscription in honour of Ptolemy II's wife, Arsinoe. The support of the pedestal is a rough assemblage of stones among which are some column fragments and blocks with hieroglyphic inscriptions. One of these blocks is now in the British Museum, and its damaged cartouche belongs most probably to Sesostris II or III; two others are inscribed for Sethos I and Psammetichus I. Immediately to the right of the pedestal can be seen the standing obelisk now in New York. The minarets and houses of the Arab town are in the distance, with the sea beyond. A Mameluke rides his horse with bow and quiver at his back; a dervish is reading to the left.

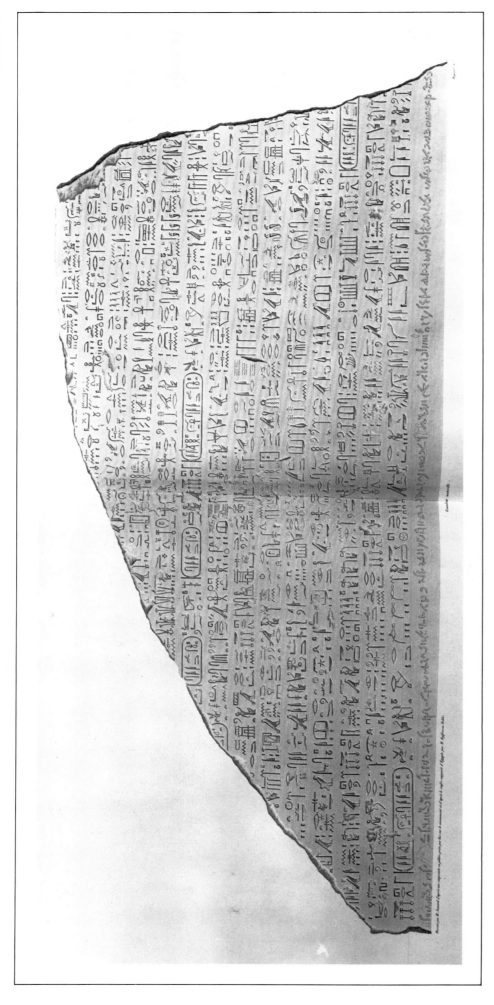

The Rosetta Stone was discovered while the French were digging by the Delta town of that name some 30 miles east of Alexandria. Its importance was guessed by Pierre Bouchard, the captain in charge of operations. The find was announced to the French Institute in Cairo, and study of the stone soon began. It was quickly realised that the three scripts might encompass only one text, and that the Greek might prove to be a translation of the two Egyptian forms of writing. The stone was ceded to Britain in 1801, and its special significance was realised by Major-General H. Turner, who was responsible for its transport to England. The frigate brought it to Deptford in the Thames and Turner requested that it should go first to the Society of Antiquaries before being lodged in the British Museum. The French were sent a plaster-cast of the stone, and the copy published here was checked in London against the original. In spite of a long-held belief that hieroglyphic writing was symbolic, perhaps mystic in nature, scholars were not slow to recognise that the repeated writing of Ptolemaios within cartouches on the stone matched the Greek for Ptolemy and was certainly alphabetic.

B ecause of erroneous theories about the hieroglyphs, it was the demotic text on the Rosetta Stone that first yielded some of its secrets. By comparing this with the Greek, the Swedish diplomat Johan Akerblad isolated all the proper names accurately. He made other sound deductions, and published an important paper on his discoveries in 1802. Further progress was impeded by his conviction that all demotic writing must be alphabetic in the manner of the proper names. The next advance in understanding the demotic text was made by Thomas Young, distinguished English physicist and physician. He realised that demotic could not be exclusively alphabetic and grasped the fact that demotic and hieroglyphics worked on similar principles. Using as basis the repetitions of the Greek text, he identified similar repetitions in the other texts. By this means he managed to equate 86 word-groups in demotic and Greek. But the real founder of Egyptian philology and of our historical knowledge was Champollion, who launched Egyptology on its proper course with his letter to M. Dacier of 1822.

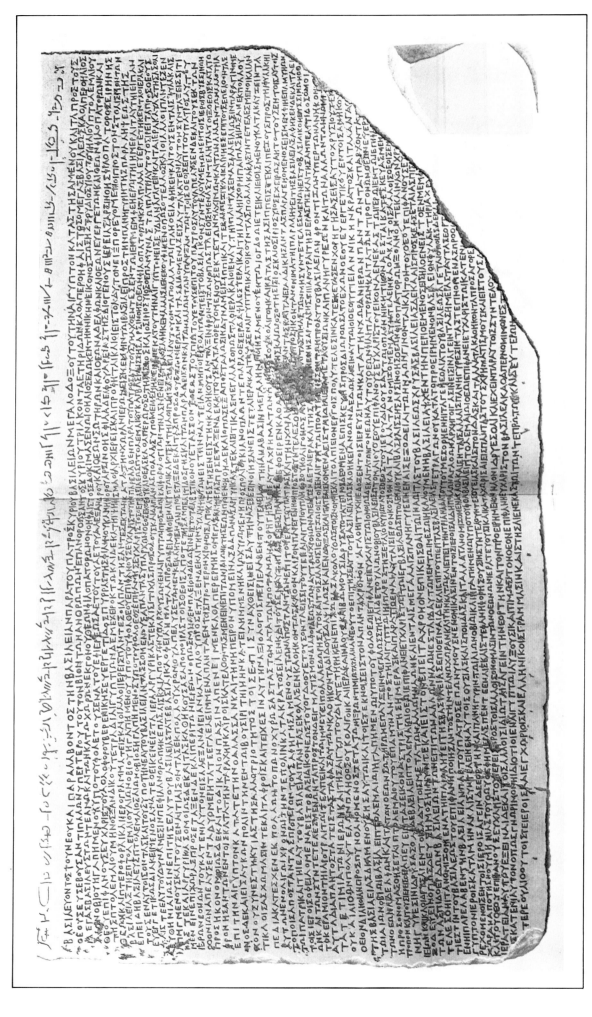

Though none of the three texts on the Rosetta Stone was complete, the Greek quickly made clear that the subject matter was a decree by the priests of Memphis. The decree was published in 196 B.C. to coincide with the first anniversary of the coronation of Ptolemy V Epiphanes. Ptolemy's benefactions were set forth, and in gratitude the priests made eight resolutions: additional honours should be accorded to the king and his predecessors; a statue of Ptolemy should be set up in each temple and worshipped thrice daily; a royal statue within a shrine should be placed in each temple sanctuary and carried in procession on certain holy days; the king's birthday and coronation day should be celebrated each month; the first five days of the month Thoth should be a special festival; priests obeying these injunctions should have a special title; private citizens should be allowed to set up a shrine for the king and keep these festivals; a stela bearing this decree in the writing of the priests, the writing of the books, and the writing of the Greeks should be placed by the statue of the king in all temples of the first, second and third class.

MEDIEVAL
AND MODERN
EGYPT

The French occupation of Egypt from July 1798 to September 1801 marks the watershed between the medieval and modern period of Egyptian history. At the time of the French expedition, Egypt had been a province of the Ottoman Empire for more than 250 years. This was an era of stagnation and decline, in which Egypt's energies were sapped by the heavy burden of taxation imposed by Constantinople and by the weakness of the ruling pashas (viceroys). The power vacuum was filled by the destructive rivalries of the Mameluke beys (lords, or high officials), into whose hands authority increasingly passed. Periodic epidemics of bubonic plague and intermittent famine reduced the country's population from an estimated eight million before the Ottoman conquest in 1517 to some three million during the 18th century. The population of Cairo suffered a comensurate decline, from perhaps half a million during its years of greatest prosperity to about 250,000 in 1798.

When the French arrived, Egypt was nominally governed by Abu Bakr Pasha, but real power lay with two Mamelukes, Murad Bey, the Emir el-Hajj (Commander of the Pilgrimage) and Ibrahim Bey, the Sheikh el-Beled (Elder of the Town). Ibrahim Bey proved only a minor nuisance to the French, following the Pasha to Syria and thereby diverting Napoleon's attention from Egypt, but Murad Bey was a sharp thorn in their flesh, obliging General Desaix to devote nine months to the unsuccessful pursuit of Murad's Mameluke army the length of Upper Egypt.

The French entered Egypt by an unorthodox and physically taxing route, landing on a barren and exposed stretch of the Mediterranean coast about eight miles west of Alexandria. Napoleon led the march through trackless desert to Alexandria, reaching its outer fortifications at 8 a.m. on 2 July. The French encountered little resistance, and were in command of the city before dusk. Alexandria was a disappointment, a small provincial town of little more than 8,000 inhabitants which bore no resemblance to the fabled city of antiquity (pls. 105-112). Napoleon remained there a week before proceeding south along the Nile to Cairo. The Mameluke army commanded by Murad Bey met the French at the so-called Battle of the Pyramids on the west bank of the Nile, in fact some distance from the pyramids at Embaba, opposite the port town of Boulaq, on 21 July 1798.

Murad's forces were no match for Napoleon's, and they fled south leaving the French to enter Cairo unopposed.

The French found Cairo vast and confusing. It had none of the regularity or formal elegance of a European capital: the streets were narrow and tortuous; there were no grand avenues or major arteries; and the innumerable quarters were sealed off from one another by gates (pl. 75). But members of the Commission of Arts and Science soon discovered that Cairo's grand houses, though they might lack outward distinction, offered at least as much comfort and luxury as those of Paris, their lush, fragrant gardens more than compensating for the cramped residential layout of Cairo (pls. 95, 97 - 101). They also encountered the extraordinary historic, social and cultural riches of the city. The painstaking study of Cairo that the Commission undertook is a model of scholarship and remains the most authoritative source of information about the city's medieval condition.

Cairo's history as a centre of human settlement predates the Arab conquest by 1000 years, but its character and development is due entirely to Islam. The nucleus of what was to become the first Arab city in Egypt was settled by the Persians in the late 6th century B.C. in the area now known as Old Cairo. There the Romans took over a fort, called by the Arabs Qasr el-Shama and now known as Babylon (pl. 67), to which with its Byzantine garrison the Arab leader Amr Ibn el-As laid siege in 641; there too the Copts built some of the earliest churches in Egypt. The first Islamic settlement, the 'camp' of Amr's troops, called Fustat, grew into the city of Misr, described by a 10th-century traveller as superior to Baghdad and larger than both Basrah and Damascus.

Cairo's development over the centuries followed the westward shifting course of the Nile and the whims of successive rulers. Ibn Tulun, who made himself the first independent ruler of Moslem Egypt in 878, quartered his troops to the north of Fustat, building the city of El-Qatai whose mosque, named after its founder, remains one of Cairo's supreme medieval legacies (pls. 78, 79). But the centre of the present-day capital was established still further north by the Fatimid general Jawhar, who invaded Egypt from Tunisia and staked out a large rectangle named El-Qahira, the 'victorious', in 969. For the 200 years of Fatimid rule El-Qahira was a palace city, head-quarters of the caliphs and their retinues; Fustat/Misr, with its Tulunid accretions, continued to be the popular and commercial centre. Both Misr and El-Qatai were destroyed as the Fatimid dynasty crumbled, and to this day the ruins of Fustat stand out as huge mounds of rubble extending from the edge of Old Cairo to the south-west rim of the Southern Cemetery.

The fortified gates of Bab el-Nasr (pl. 81) and Bab el-Futuh to the north and Bab Zuwaila to the south mark the former limits of the Fatimid enclosure. Within the walls were two vast palaces, long since destroyed, between which ran a street which has withstood subsequent urban redevelopment and remains the principal artery from Bab el-Futuh to Bab Zuwaila. Plague, famine, earthquake and the Crusaders brought an end to Fatimid rule and opened the royal enclosure of El-Qahira to invasion by the population of Fustat/Misr. When the Ayyubid governor Salah el-Din (Saladin) imposed his authority over Egypt in 1171, he made it his first task to fortify the Citadel (pl. 82) and extend the city walls to encompass the former Tulunid quarter. It was within this expanded area that Cairo's architects and craftsmen created, between 1171 and 1517, the monuments that earned 14th-century Cairo such tributes as those of the Moroccan Ibn Batutah, who acclaimed Egypt's capital as the 'mother of cities..., boundless in multitudes of buildings, peerless in beauty and splendour', and the Tunisian Ibn Khaldun, for whom Cairo was 'the metropolis of the universe, garden of the world, swarming core of the human species..., a city embellished with castles and palaces, bedecked with convents and colleges, illuminated by the moons and stars of knowledge'. An Italian visitor in 1138 estimated that the city of Cairo had a population greater than all Tuscany.

The boundaries of Cairo at the time of the French expedition were virtually those established by Salah el-Din. Most of the area between the Nile and the Nasiri Canal, dug by order of Sultan el-Nasir Mohamed in the early 14th century and running from south to north parallel with the main canal and west of present-day Bab el-Luk and Ezbekiya Square, was undrained marsh. Boulaq, the port of Cairo, was a self-contained town separated from the capital by an agricultural plain (pl. 102); Old Cairo was similarly independent, south of the ruin fields of Fustat. The urban plan and socio-economic organisation of the city was based essentially on trade and profession. All this changed dramatically and irreversibly with the modernisation of Egypt launched by Mohamed Ali shortly after the departure of the French and accelerated by his khedival successors. With the rapid growth of Cairo's population during the last 20 years, more and more of the city's medieval buildings have disappeared, and the few remaining traces of its glorious past are hemmed in by high-rise blocks and elevated highways. The threat to their existence is acknowledged by the Egyptian government, which in 1979 invited UNESCO to place the Old City on the World Heritage list. There is thus some reason to hope that the finest surviving monuments admired and recorded so comprehensively by the French may be preserved for future generations.

HILARY WEIR

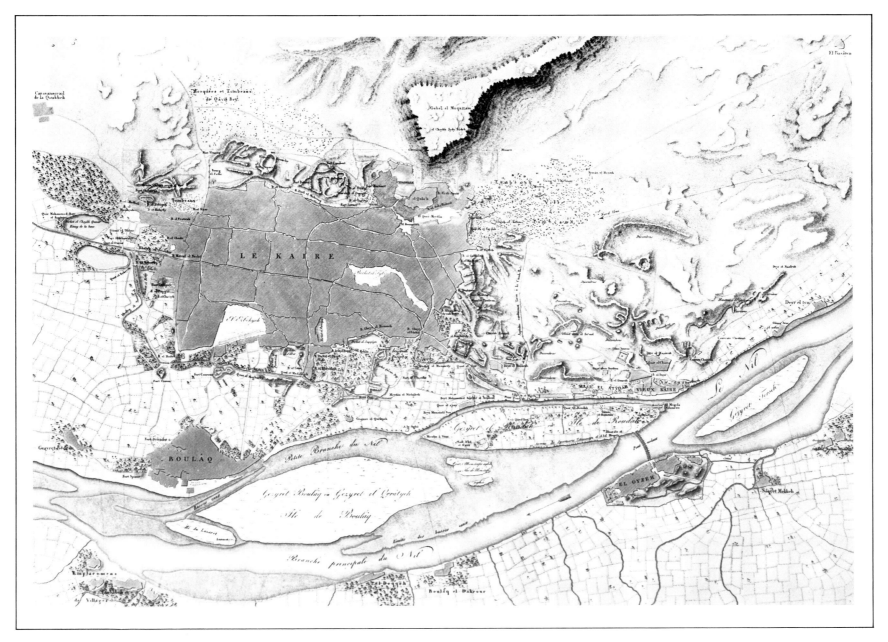

The French expedition produced the first accurately-scaled map of Cairo. Edmé-François Jomard, the savant charged with the task, worked without a day's interruption for two months, assisted by an interpreter, a public scrivener who knew the city intimately, and three or four other guides. Jomard found Cairo baffling. 'Not only are its streets and public squares extremely irregular, but -- with the exception of a few major arteries -- the city is almost entirely composed of very short streets and twisting alleys, with innumerable dead-ends. Each of these sections is closed by a gate, which the inhabitants open when they wish; as a result the interior of Cairo is very difficult to know as a whole.' Jomard's minutely annotated map remains an indispensable source of information about the street plan, population, buildings and economic organisation of medieval Cairo. This small-scale 'plan' shows the city of Cairo proper (the irregular shaded rectangle) in relation to other centres of population: Boulaq, Old Cairo and Giza. The shape of most of the islands in the Nile has altered since the map was drawn. Virtually the entire area is now part of the dense urban metropolis of greater Cairo.

PLATE 76   NILOMETER ON RODA ISLAND

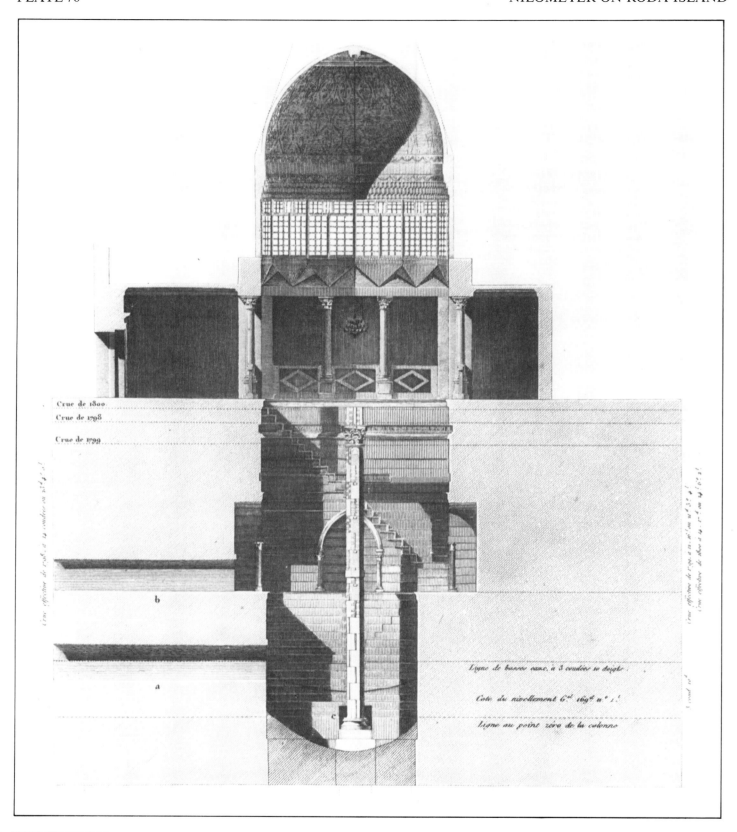

The Nilometer stands on the southern tip of Roda island, close to the east bank of the Nile. Roda means 'meadow', and until the 20th century the island was barely inhabited. Jomard describes the avenue of sycamores leading to the Nilometer, and the grove of orange and lemon trees in which it stood. There was probably a nilometer on this site in ancient times. The present structure dates from A.D. 861 and is the oldest Islamic and sole surviving Abbasid monument in Cairo. It is surmounted by a domed kiosk erected in the Ottoman period, lined with Turkish tiles. The Nilometer itself consists of a stone-lined pit descending well below the surface of the Nile, from which three tunnels lead at different heights. The water level was measured against a central column, marked off in cubits. When the water reached a height of 16 cubits the signal was given to cut the dyke at the mouth of Cairo's principal canal (see pl. 93). Forty-three steps lead down from the entrance to the upper tunnel, whose bays are formed by pointed arches, a feature not introduced in Europe until three centuries later.

On 2 December 1798 Napoleon reviewed his cavalry on the Qubbeh plain, and determined that they were sufficiently well mounted and well equipped to take on the Mamelukes. Qubbeh lies a short distance to the north-east of Cairo on the edge of the eastern desert, and was undeveloped until the 19th century. It is now part of metropolitan Cairo. The plain was the site of two great battles. It was here that in 1517 the Turkish Sultan Selim I defeated the Mamelukes and made Egypt part of the Ottoman Empire. And on 20 March 1800 General Kléber, commander of the French armies after Napoleon's departure for France in August 1799, met and beat back a Turkish army of 40,000 and briefly recaptured Lower Egypt. In 1863 the Khedive Ismail built a huge palace at Qubbeh, set in a large park. Today this palace is used for state visitors, amongst whom was the late Shah of Iran, who stayed there until his death in 1980.

PLATE 78   IBN TULUN MOSQUE

Jomard considered the mosque of Ahmed Ibn Tulun, 'built between 877 and 879 by the first sultan of Egypt', the oldest of all Cairo's mosques. He is essentially correct, for although the mosque of Amr Ibn el-As in Fustat / Misr (on the edge of Old Cairo) was founded two centuries earlier, its present fabric is much altered from the original, whereas that of Ibn Tulun is virtually unchanged. Ibn Tulun was governor of Egypt under the Abbasid caliphs who ruled the Moslem world from Iraq. Arriving with a large army, he established a palace quarter, El-Qatai, north of the city of Fustat. His mosque is the largest as well as the oldest in Cairo, covering an area of six and a half acres. The huge expanse of its open courtyard was determined by the need to accommodate Ibn Tulun's army at prayer time. The perspective chosen by the artist allows only a glimpse of the mosque's principal and unparalleled feature, its graceful parapet crenellations which have been compared to a chain of paper dolls. The viewpoint is that of the 'ziyada', or precinct, separating the mosque from the bazaars and other secular buildings of the quarter. To the left is the entrance to the minaret, whose boat-shaped weather-vane seems to have interested the artist more than its unique square base, circular upper storey and external winding stair, which are almost certainly of Samarran inspiration. The horseshoe arch visible in the distance is part of the bridge connecting the minaret to the roof of the mosque.

The mosque of Ibn Tulun has been much restored but little altered since its foundation. Of classic courtyard style, it is surrounded by rows of arcades, deeper on the sanctuary (qibla , or Mecca-facing) side than along the other walls. Built of stucco-(plaster-)covered brick, this mosque was inspired by the architecture of the princely state of Samarra in Iraq, 9th-century capital of the Abbasid caliphate that despatched Ibn Tulun to Egypt. The outermost sanctuary arcade stretches away to the left in the picture, its deep shade contrasting with the glare of sunshine in the open court and other arcades. The pointed arches rest on piers with engaged pilasters at each corner, of which the stucco capitals are carved with stylised grape and vine-leaf motifs. The arches are outlined and underlined by decorative stucco friezes of geometric and floral design; above and between are smaller arches flanked by roundels. The structure in the centre of the court is the ablutions fountain, built in 1296. The crenellations visible along the rim of its square base no longer exist. The mosque is today the sole surviving evidence of the luxurious quarter built by Ibn Tulun, complete with palace and 'maydan' (polo field or square) as well as the mosque.

PLATE 80   HAKIM MOSQUE

This mosque, whose gaping arches and uneven courtyard testify to centuries of neglect, is that of the Fatimid caliph El-Hakim, notorious for the eccentricities and cruelties of his 25-year reign. Succeeding to the caliphate in 996 at the age of 11, El-Hakim visited upon his subjects measures of calculated brutality in the name of vigilance: amongst his edicts was one forbidding cobblers to make shoes for women, to enforce his view that women should stay at home. In 1021 he proclaimed himself divine. Shortly after, he disappeared while riding his donkey on the Moqattam Hills at night. His body was never found. Most presume him murdered, but the Druze -- who take their name from El-Hakim's chief theologian, El-Darezi -- believe that he will reappear to inaugurate the millennium. El-Hakim's mosque, built between 990 and 1013, follows Ibn Tulun's in congregational plan and scale (see pl. 79). It lay outside the northern limit of the original city walls, erected by the Fatimid conquerors of Egypt and founders of El-Qahira (Cairo) in 969. The cylindrical upper sections of its massive square-based minarets were rebuilt after an earthquake in 1303. Even before the earthquake, El-Hakim's mosque suffered mixed fortunes, being used as a prison for Crusader captives during the 12th century and then as a stable. Five centuries later, when Napoleon conquered Egypt, the mosque served as a military warehouse; at the turn of the present century it housed Cairo's first public collection of Islamic art, and thereafter a school. In November 1980 the mosque was reopened by President Sadat following its total renovation by the Bohra sect, an Ismaili group based in India who claim spiritual descent from the Fatimid Imams and revere El-Hakim.

Bab el-Nasr, the 'gate of victory', is -- with nearby Bab el-Futuh, 'the gate of conquests' -- one of the world's outstanding examples of pre-Crusader military architecture. Jomard pronounced Bab el-Nasr 'the premier monument of Cairo' in style and taste. Both gates date from 1087, when the Armenian General Badr el-Gamali, governor of Acre under the caliph Mustansir, strengthened Cairo's defences against possible attack by the Seljuk Turks of Syria and extended the wall to incorporate El-Hakim's mosque (see pl. 80). Attack never came, but the city's northern fortifications remain to demonstrate the power of the Shia dynasty that ruled Egypt for two centuries and the skill of the Armenian architects who introduced to Moslem Cairo the idea and technique of building in stone. The earlier buildings of El-Qahira, like those of Fustat / Misr and El-Qatai, were made of brick, as were the original walls erected by the Fatimids in 969. Bab el-Nasr's rubble core is faced with finely dressed limestone. Its arch is Romano-Byzantine in style, and on the flat-fronted flanking towers are round (Roman) and oblong (Arab) shields. Several blocks used in the construction were taken from very much older buildings and include fragments of ancient Egyptian reliefs and hieroglyphs. The towers were occupied by Napoleon's troops, who carved their commanders' names into the fabric: 'Tour Julien' and 'Tour Corbin' remind contemporary visitors of the French expedition. The French also reinforced the upper storey, filling in the ragged crenellations. From Bab el-Nasr's western tower one looks down into El-Hakim's mosque, whose eastern wall lies just behind the façade projecting into the left foreground of the illustration.

B uilt on a spur of the Moqattam Hills and rising sheer above the city, Cairo's citadel was one of the greatest medieval fortresses and dominates the skyline to this day. Ibn Tulun and other early rulers favoured the site as a place to take the air, but its strategic potential was developed by Salah el-Din (Saladin), Islam's defender against the Crusader armies, in the late 12th century. Most of the buildings in this view post-date Salah el-Din by several hundred years. To the left, outside the citadel precincts, stands the 16th-century mosque of El-Mahmudiya; like the flanking towers of 18th-century Bab el-Azab, one of the citadel's five exterior gates, it is painted red and white. Bab el-Azab leads into the narrow lane between high walls in which, in 1811, Mohamed Ali massacred the Mameluke Beys as they left the banquet to which he had invited them. Thereafter Mohamed Ali's power was absolute, and by 1824 he had demolished most of the buildings on the summit of the citadel in order to erect his grandiose mosque, whose multiple domes and twin 'pencil' minarets are now Cairo's most familiar landmark.

The citadel was the seat of government and official residence of Egypt's rulers from the time of Salah el-Din's nephew, Malik el-Kamil (1218-38), until the mid-19th century. Its imposing walls enclosed a multitude of military and civil buildings, dating from every period. Jomard explains that the citadel was divided into three enclosures, each defended by strong crenellated towers and resembling a self-contained town. The Bab el-Gebel ('gate of the mountain') and Moqattam Tower of this illustration stand at the south-east end of the northern enclosure, fronting the Moqattam Hills, and date from the 16th/17th centuries. At the time of the French expedition the citadel housed 12 mosques, 14 wells (one of which could store water sufficient for 10,000 men for a year), five interior gates, 32 towers and a public bath, in addition to the ruler's palace, the ceremonial hall (Divan of Joseph, see pl. 84), harems, the mint, barracks, military arsenal, shops and markets. From the citadel extends a vista which Jomard pronounced beyond the skill of an artist to depict. Though marred nowadays by pollution, the view still encompasses the chain of pyramids in the western desert, the dense cultivation of the Nile valley, the river itself, and the urban panorama of Cairo.

PLATE 84

PALACE OR MOSQUE ON THE CITADEL

This imposing edifice was demolished, together with many other structures, to make way for Mohamed Ali's mosque and palace in the early 19th century. Jomard says that it was the largest building on the citadel, a palace or mosque named after Salah el-Din Yusuf (Joseph), who first fortified the citadel in 1171. He speculates that the 32 red granite columns of its 'hypostyle' hall were brought from Babylon (Old Cairo) or Alexandria; whatever their exact provenance they must indeed belong to the pharaonic or Ptolemaic period of Egyptian history. The building had been abandoned by the time of the French expedition, as suggested by the spreading mounds and passage of baggage trains across the floor. The other monument bearing the name of Salah el-Din, 'Joseph's Well', was still functioning in Jomard's time and may be visited today. It lies just south of one of the citadel's other surviving medieval structures, the mosque of El-Nasir Mohamed (1335), not far from the Moqattam Tower (pl. 83), and was excavated by 'an incalculable number' of Crusader prisoners in the 1170s, according to a contemporary witness. Jomard estimates its depth at about 300 feet, the level of the Nile and the water table.

The mosque of Sultan Hasan is to many 20th-century connoisseurs, as it was to Jomard in 1798, one of the most beautiful monuments in Cairo and 'in the first rank of Arab architectural works'. It was built in the mid-14th century, and its grandeur of scale remains unequalled. It is difficult today to obtain an unimpeded view, for the mosque is now jostled by other buildings and by the traffic congestion of Salah el-Din square (shown in the foreground of pl. 82) at the foot of the citadel. The small houses against the mosque have however been removed. Sultan Hasan reigned from 1345, when he was 12, until he was imprisoned by one of his emirs in 1361. His vast monument includes a cruciform 'madrasa' or theological college, a domed mausoleum, and accommodation (long since unused) for about 500 teachers and students. The dome of the mausoleum was rebuilt in the Ottoman period, as was the lower of the two minarets. The other minaret is older, and at 283 feet is the highest in Cairo.

PLATE 86

SULTAN HASAN MOSQUE

This view does little justice to the single most remarkable feature of Sultan Hasan's mosque: its towering and elaborately sculpted 85-foot entrance. Some impression of the height of this 'porch' can be gained from the diminutive size of the human figures at its foot, but the tiers of stalactites rising to a shell niche surrounded by bands of Koranic inscription are partly obscured by the shadow and by the angle from which it has been drawn. The façade is austere, offering no clue to the rich variety of the interior. The minaret dates from the late 17th century. The building on the right has been demolished; in its place is the neo-Mameluke mosque of El-Rifa'i, built between 1870 and 1911 as a mausoleum for the Egyptian royal family. Here lie the Khedive Ismail, King Fuad and others of their line. In 1980 the late Shah of Iran was interred alongside them.

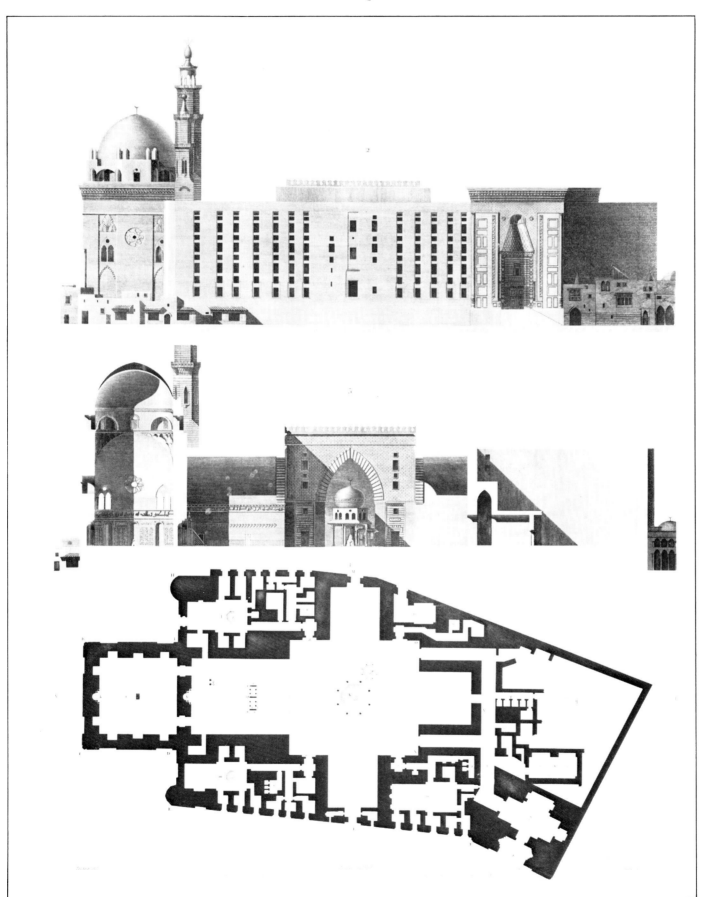

The colossal scale of the mosque of Sultan Hasan is clearly demonstrated by the elevation drawing. The façade measures 165 yards by 75, its severity relieved only by narrow vertical bays. The walls are crowned by a honeycomb cornice; most of its surmounting fleur-de-lys crenellations were removed, except around the mausoleum, during the Ottoman period. The great entrance portal is offset from the rest of the façade at a 30 degree angle, as shown in the plan. It was to have been given greater dramatic emphasis by two surmounting minarets, but construction of the second was abandoned after the first fell in 1360, killing 300 people. The plan reveals how the Mameluke-period architects contrived to adjust the essential features of their monuments to the irregular exterior configuration dictated by Cairo's existing buildings and streets: the relationship of the portal to the rest of the façade was probably determined more by the need to respect the available building plot than by any desire to innovate.

PLATE 88

DETAILS OF SULTAN HASAN MOSQUE

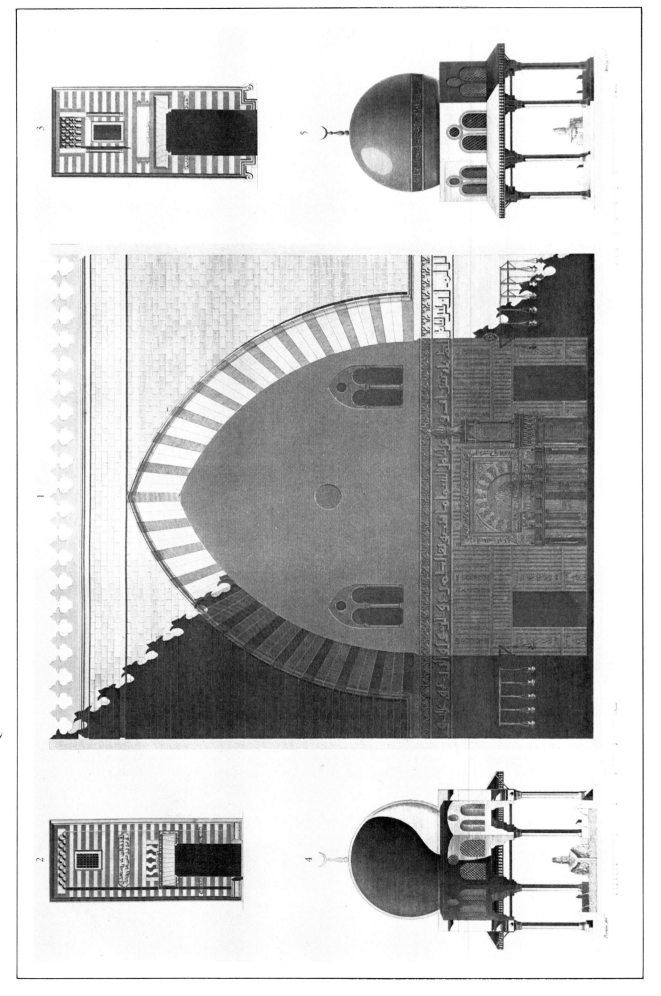

T he entrance portal of Sultan Hasan's mosque leads into a lofty and richly-decorated vestibule, then through bare and ill-lit corridors out into the dazzling brilliance of the open central court. Four immense vaulted 'iwans' (arched bays) surround the court; the arch of the sanctuary iwan, shown in this illustration (no. 1), is the biggest in Cairo, and its recessed walls are panelled with coloured marble surmounted by a band of Koranic inscription in commanding Kufic style. Flanking the iwans are doors leading from the court to the students' accommodation (nos. 2, 3). The doors are framed with alternating courses of black and white marble, their lintels 'joggled'. That on the left is especially remarkable, for the joggling is no veneer but interlocks like a three-dimensional jigsaw. The pavilion over the ablutions fountain in the centre of the court (nos. 4, 5) is thought to date from the Ottoman period. The bulbous stucco-covered wooden dome rests on an octagonal drum, in turn supported by a wooden canopy upheld by octagonal marble pillars.

Jomard remarks on the 'prodigious' variety of coloured marble and ornament, the large multicoloured calligraphy in blue, gold, red and green, and the multitude of lamps suspended from the vaults of the dome of Sultan Hasan's mauso- leum. He quotes with approval Cairo's medieval topographer, El-Maqrizi (1364-1442): 'Islam does not possess another temple that can compare with the college of Sultan Hasan for the height and grandeur of its design and the beauty of its architecture'. These characteristics are particularly evident in the 'mihrab' (prayer niche, no. 5) with its double co- lumns, marble marquetry and Koranic inscription. It is surpris- ing that the artist did not choose to illustrate the magnificent south-east door from the sanctuary into the mausoleum: perhaps its silver and gold-inlaid bronze was overlaid with grime in 1798 and did not catch his eye. His attention seems rather to have been drawn to the detail of capital and column, the variety of ornament, the sculp- tural quality of the different struc- tures within the mosque, notably the 'dikka' (platform; nos. 2 and 3), ablutions fountain (no. 1), 'minbar' (pulpit; no. 4) and 'mihrab' (no. 5).

PLATE 90

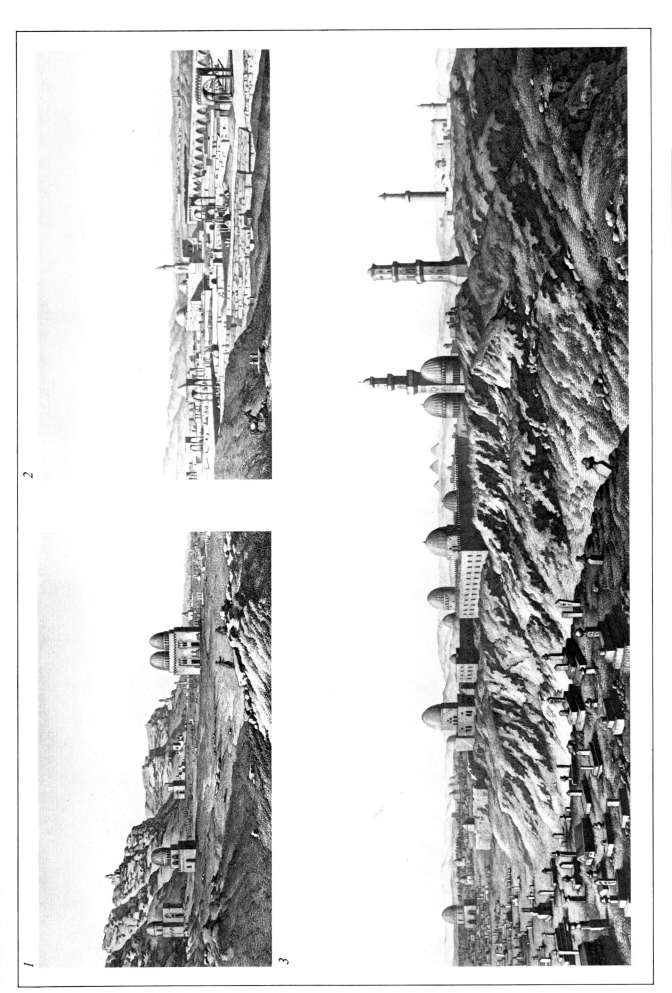

C airo's vast 'cities of the dead' struck the French as forcibly as later visitors. The northern or eastern cemetery stretches for more than a mile north and east of the citadel; the southern, for a similar distance to the south. Jomard observed that the necropolis was equivalent in extent to a quarter of the city of Cairo. The southern cemetery or Great Qarafa, seen in these illustrations, was the necropolis of Fustat/Misr and contains the tombs of some of Cairo's earlier rulers and saints, as well as many tombs dating from the Mameluke and later periods. Intersected by the 14th-century aqueduct (part of which is visible in no. 2) and 20th-century traffic artery of Salah Salem, the cemetery lies immediately below the Moqattam Hills (no. 1), on the summit of which stands the Fatimid mosque of El-Giyushi or Badr el-Gamali, builder of Cairo's north wall (see pl. 81); it boasts the oldest surviving minaret in Cairo. The most famous shrines in the Great Qarafa are those of the Moslem saints Imam Shafei, descendant of the Prophet's uncle, who died in 820; Sayyida Nafisa, a direct descendant of the Prophet, who emigrated to Cairo from the Hijaz and died in 824; and Sayyida Ruqayya, daughter of the fourth caliph Ali. The mausoleums all post-date their deaths. One of Egypt's lesser-known female rulers, Shagaret el-Dur, who reigned briefly in 1250, is also buried here, in a mausoleum built to her command.

F rom a distance the cities of the dead appear as a forest of minarets and domes. The earliest Moslem tombs in Cairo were canopies with four piers or pillars supporting a dome, usually built of brick. The spaces between the piers were later filled in, forming a square base supporting a transitional zone upon which was set the drum of the dome. Early domes were made of brick, plastered and decorated, sometimes ribbed; during the Mameluke period domes were built of stone, carved in zigzag or elaborate arabesque designs. The cenotaphs within the tomb chambers vary from plain wood or stone construction to the exaggerated decoration of the 19th century. The head of the tomb is marked by a pillar, sometimes topped by a bulb representing the turban. As Jomard noted, the Egyptians regularly visit the tombs of their family dead on Fridays, bringing food and enjoying a picnic within the precinct, a practice which some believe derives from the pharaonic preoccupation with the afterlife.

PLATE 92   CAIRO AQUEDUCT

Originally built by Sultan El-Nasir Mohamed in the early 14th century, the aqueduct had to be extended several times in order to follow the westward-shifting course of the Nile. The massive hexagonal intake tower was built by Sultan El-Ghuri in 1505. The aqueduct carried water a distance of nearly two miles from the Nile to the base of the citadel, and was a principal source of Cairo's water supply until 1872. The channel of the aqueduct is borne on a series of pointed arches, and water was raised into it from the Nile by enormous water-wheels turned by oxen. Much of the aqueduct has survived, although it is pierced by roads at many points.

The ancient ceremony of the opening of the dyke was the greatest of all medieval Egyptian festivals. The illustration depicts the ceremony of August 1799, which is described in detail by Jomard. French officers raise the tricolor on the roof of the aqueduct intake tower which stood beside the mouth of the Khalig el-Misri (Egyptian canal), which for centuries divided Cairo into two unequal parts and was one of its principal sources of water. When the height of the Nile as registered by the Nilometer on Roda island (see pl. 76) had reached more than 16 cubits, the earth dyke blocking the mouth of the Khalig was removed; throughout the Nile valley dykes were unblocked and the annual inundation permitted to spread across the land, transforming it into a 'vast sea dotted by islets'. The festival began at sunset, when illuminated barges sailed up the narrow branch of the Nile between the east bank, near Old Cairo, and Roda island. At sunrise, to the accompaniment of cannon and musket fire, music and the hubbub of huge crowds gathered on high ground near the mouth of the Khalig, the dyke was breached; men hurled themselves towards the pavilion to scrabble for coins thrown by the Agha and other dignitaries. Within ten minutes the water level was established; within an hour, the inflow reached the centre of Cairo, filling the lakes fronting its most elegant squares. The celebrations continued far into the night, with fireworks and music and processions of illuminated boats.

PLATE 94

EZBEKIYA

E zbekiya, developed by the Emir Ezbak in the late 15th century, was in 1798 the largest square in Cairo; Jomard estimated that the Place Louis XV could be fitted into it three times. During the annual inundation the square was filled with several feet of water, which Jomard pronounced most picturesque at night when Cairo's notables would relax in illuminated barges before their houses and palaces around the shores. From its inception Ezbekiya was Cairo's most elegant quarter. Mohamed Ali converted the lake into formal gardens in the early 19th century; thereafter, Ezbekiya became the business and tourist centre of Cairo. It is still the principal business district, and the vestiges of the gardens survive, though bisected by one of Cairo's busiest traffic arteries, 26 July Street.

The most sumptuous palace in Ezbekiya Square (above), Cairo's most prosperous and fashionable quarter (see pl. 94), was built by Alfi Bey just before the French expedition. Its owner fled to Upper Egypt, and Napoleon promptly commandeered the palace for his headquarters. Later, the palace briefly housed a language school, until in 1849 Samuel Shepheard was given permission to use it as an hotel. Such was the demand from tourists that he demolished the palace in 1862 and in its place constructed a new Shepheard's, for decades one of the world's most celebrated hotels. It was burned down during the anti-British riots of 1952, and its present-day namesake stands not in Ezbekiya Square but on the Nile Corniche in Garden City. The El-Tor caravan (below) brought coal from Sinai and merchandise imported from Arabia and the East via Qulzum (Suez, pl. 123). Cairo's medieval prosperity was very largely based on its strategic position in east-west trade. Until Vasco da Gama discovered the Cape route in 1498, a principal trade route from China to the West ran by way of Jedda across the Red Sea, either to Qossair and across to the Nile near Luxor (see pl. 122) or to Suez and overland to Cairo, thence down the Nile to the Mediterranean. The Suez route continued to be used by caravans until the 20th century, and – in reverse -- by Moslems making the pilgrimage to Mecca.

PLATE 96   BIRKET EL-FIL

B irket el-Fil, 'the pond of the Elephant' (because of its shape), was one of several palatial districts that grew up along the banks of natural lakes formed by the flood waters of the Nile. Between the mosque of Ibn Tulun and the mosque of Sultan Hasan, the quarter covers the ruins of the former Tulunid city of El-Qatai, destroyed by the Abbasids in 905 and undeveloped until the 14th century. Emirs and other notables built palaces around the lake and endowed theological colleges (madrasas) and monasteries (khankas) along the main route leading to the citadel, Sharia Saliba. The lake was filled in during the 19th century.

The house of Osman Bey, like so many of Cairo's grand mansions, has long since disappeared. Seen here across its central courtyard, the building presents many features characteristic of the medieval period: a porticoed arcade resting on marble columns; projecting upper storeys with wooden lattice-work (mashrabiya) grills to screen the ladies of the house from inquisitive eyes; a wind vent (malqaf) on the roof, open to the north to conduct cool breezes into the interior; and accommodation sufficient for a substantial retinue as well as livestock. Jomard observed that the great houses of Cairo bore little resemblance to European palaces, but that they were nonetheless not devoid of sumptuous elegance. He found their interior plan too irregular to describe, remarking only that the rooms were often at different levels. The large ground-floor room (qa'a) was paved with marble; often with a central sunken area with a fountain. The main furnishings were large sofas or divans, rich carpets and other materials and numerous cushions. Jomard noticed the presence of Japanese vases among other ornaments and utensils.

PLATE 98   HOUSE OF HASAN KACHEF

The house of Hasan Kachef, one of the Mamelukes who fled with Murad Bey to Upper Egypt after the battle of the Pyramids in 1798, was commandeered by the French and occupied by the Institut de l'Egypte. Created by decree on 22 August 1798, the Institute's president was Gaspard Monge, here seen welcoming the vice-president, Napoleon himself to the inaugural meeting. There were 37 members, divided among four sections. The Institute produced the Description de l'Egypte, including the first detailed map of the country. It also assembled the first library of Egyptology, housed in this building. The meeting room of the Institute was the 'harem' or women's quarters on the first floor of the house. The central lantern admitting light supports a dome. The building no longer exists.

The entrance to the house of Hasan Kachef is solid and imposing rather than grand, typical of the style of the period which minimised exterior ornament. The front door would have led into a twisting corridor designed so that passers-by could not glimpse the interior. Beneath the intricate 'mashrabiya' (lattice-work) of the overhanging upper-floor windows is a carved frieze of decorative medallions; above, a projecting wooden canopy affords extra protection from the heat. The rectangular structure on the roof is the wind vent, open to cool breezes from the north. Another view of the courtyard of this house shows an imposing sundial bearing the legend 'L'AN VII RF (République Française)'. This was erected by a member of the Institute to record the new republican or revolutionary calendar.

PLATE 100

HOUSE OF QASIM BEY

T his grand house has not survived. Qasim Bey, like Hasan Kachef and Alfi Bey (for their mansions see pls. 98, 99, 95), fled from Napoleon; his house was taken over by the Commission of Arts and Science. Among its 165 members were civil engineers, cartographers, surveyors, astronomers, botanists, surgeons, antiquarians, mineralogists, chemists, and zoologists, who travelled the length of Egypt with the French army, observing and recording virtually every aspect of its history, geography and customs. The Commission installed a printing press (the first in Egypt), workshops and a zoo on its premises. The results of its labours were incorporated in the Description. This plate reveals the elaborate design and sumptuous decoration of the mansions of wealthy Ottoman-period beys.

This house, which has not survived, belonged to Soliman Agha. The French authors of the Description made the point that in Cairo there was no mansion to display such luxury as might occur in a great European town house. But they were struck by the richness of carpets and tapestries, the intricacy of woodwork and mosaic, and the decorative use of tiles, as seen in this impressive 'qa'a' (reception room). And usually there was the gentle play of a fountain, to cool the senses and refresh the mind. The arched recesses, marble panels and pavement, and richly-painted lantern were typical of the period.

PLATE 102   MOSQUE IN BOULAQ

The Sinaniya mosque in Boulaq was built in 1573 by Sinan Pasha, governor of Egypt under Selim II. It still stands today. Quintessentially Ottoman and un-Cairene in style, the Sinaniya's huge dome is supported by a 16-sided drum resting on a square base and surrounded by arcades with domed vaults. The 'pencil' minaret bears no resemblance to the multi-storeyed structures of the Mameluke period. At the time of the French expedition, Boulaq had a population of about 24,000 and was the port of Cairo, separated from the city by a wide agricultural plain. Boulaq's development began in the 15th century when Sultan Barsbay established monopolies in certain goods and required Red Sea trade to travel overland from Qulzum (Suez, pl. 123) to Boulaq. During the Ottoman period Boulaq was the principal loading and unloading point for merchandise to and from the east, Africa, Upper and Lower Egypt, the Mediterranean and the west. Jomard lists cotton, linen, henna, sugar, rice, saffron and natron among the Egyptian goods traded through Boulaq, and remarks that the port had 24 mosques and a great many 'wakala' (warehouses and commercial inns). Boulaq is now an integral part of Cairo.

Nasryeh Gate, seen here and included by Jomard in his list of the 13 most important of Cairo's 61 gates, no longer exists. The Nasryeh was 'in the west towards the Nile', in that section of modern Cairo's Abdin quarter traversed by Sharia El-Nasriya, near whose junction with Sharia Port Said stands the only house occupied by the French Commission of Arts and Science to have survived into the 1980s (Beit Ibrahim Katkhuda el-Sinnari). The district was adorned by one of Cairo's many lakes, and a canal excavated during the reign of Sultan el-Nasir Mohamed (early 14th century) encouraged the development of this part of the city. The view appears to be from north-west to south-east, perhaps across the Sayyida Zeinab quarter in which one or two buildings dating from the 18th century or earlier remain, towards the Moqattam Hills. Jomard writes in almost lyrical terms about the 'many beautiful gardens' in and around Cairo, so different from those in Paris, with their luxuriant groves of orange and lemon trees, vines, acacia, sycamore, myrtle, huge-leaved bananas, mulberries, pomegranates, and soaring date palms.

PLATE 104 HOUSE OF MURAD BEY; BRIDGE OF BOATS; AVENUE OF SYCAMORES

1

2

The evening after his victory at the battle of the Pyramids, fought on 21 July 1798 at Embaba on the west bank of the Nile several miles north of the Giza pyramids, Napoleon repaired to the country house (no. 1) of his opponent Murad Bey, who had retreated south with part of the Mameluke army. Giza was a small town on the west bank of the Nile, where Murad Bey preferred to live in relative isolation from the life of the capital. Napoleon found that the house bore no resemblance to a European palace, but his officers were impressed by its rich furniture and especially by a large vine trellis, covered with heavy grapes, in the spacious garden. Scene 2 shows the bridge of boats connecting the north of Roda island with the east bank of the Nile; the buildings south of the bridge are part of the country house of Napoleon's other opponent, Ibrahim Bey, who shared supremacy with Murad. In the distance is the aqueduct (see pl. 92). The final illustration (no. 3) shows part of the avenue of sycamores leading to the Nilometer, looking west across the Nile towards the pyramids.

3

Alexandria was Egypt's capital for almost 1000 years. The ancient city filled the whole area between the Mediterranean and Lake Mareotis. It was bisected by two principal streets: the Canopic Way, which ran from the Gate of the Moon in the west to the Gate of the Sun (Porte Rosette) in the east; and the Street of Soma (tomb) which ran south-north, from the lake harbour to the Great Harbour (Port Neuf). Parts of these two streets are followed by present-day Tariq el-Horiyya and Sharia Nebi Daniel. There are few traces of the ancient city's celebrated marble monuments. 'Pompey's Pillar' in south-west Alexandria stands on the former citadel of Rhakotis, not far from the 2nd-century A.D. cemetery of Kom el-Shukafa, known as the Catacombs and on the site of the Temple of Serapis. The 15th-century fort of Qaitbey occupies the north-east tip of Pharos island, the site of the legendary lighthouse which commanded the entrance to the Great Harbour. The 'modern town' of 1798 was confined to the neck of land between the two harbours. A Roman theatre and bath-house complex was found in the 1960s at Kom el-Dikka, just outside the Arab walls to the north-east. Further east, covering the whole promontory of Silsila (whose northernmost point is shown on the map as Pharillon), lay the royal enclosure. The Mouseion, which was the foremost centre of learning and largest library of antiquity, probably adjoined this complex.

PLATE 106   WALLS OF ALEXANDRIA

The Arab conquerors of Egypt in 642 admired and occupied Alexandria, but altered Egypt's focus, transferring its capital back inland, its principal lines of communication to Arabia and the east rather than the Mediterranean and the north. Alexandria's prosperity and population declined. The Arab walls built in the 9th century and shown on the French plan (pl. 105) enclosed only a small section of the Greek and Roman city. The French found them in bad repair, though noted that some of the many towers flanking the walls were massive and well built. But by 1798 even the Arab city was deserted. Within the fortified area lay nothing but the ruins of the ancient capital, together with the tombs and abandoned dwellings from the Arab period. There were two monasteries, a synagogue and several mosques, including one called 'St. Athanasius' (present day Attarine) which occupied the site of the church named after Alexandria's great 4th-century bishop and patriarch. The 18th-century population lived on the neck of land between the 'island' of Pharos and the mainland (see pl. 105). This is no natural feature, but the accumulation of centuries of silt around the narrow causeway built at the time of Alexandria's foundation to connect Pharos with the continent. The causeway was called the Heptastadium, because it was seven 'stadia' long (about a mile altogether). Pharos island is known today as Ras el-Tin, its western section occupied by the vast palace built on the site of 19th-century structures by King Fuad in the 1920s.

PLATE 107

The Castle of Pharos, Fort Qaitbey, was constructed by Sultan Qaitbey in the late 15th century to counter the Ottoman threat. It stands on the eastern tip of the promontory commanding the entrance to the New or Eastern Harbour (known in antiquity as the 'Great' harbour), on the site of the famous Pharos lighthouse, one of the seven wonders of the ancient world. Thought to have been built in the reign of Ptolemy II Philadelphus (285-246 B.C.), the Pharos was surrounded by a colonnaded court and had four storeys: square, octagonal, circular, and the lantern, which was surmounted by an enormous statue of Poseidon. Its height was some 500 feet, and its light could be seen for 80 miles out to sea. The Pharos was still largely intact at the time of the Arab conquest. Ibn Tulun carried out some essential restoration work in the 10th century; but later rulers were unable to repair the damage caused by earthquakes in 1100, when the octagonal storey was dislodged, and 1307, when the entire structure was destroyed. Fort Qaitbey was an irregular pentagon, enclosing a square castle which incorporated a mosque. The French found in one of its upper chambers a quantity of Crusader swords and other weapons. The fort was badly damaged by the British bombardment in 1822, but it has since been partly restored and now houses a naval museum. The view top right shows the so-called 'Diamond Rock' with the castle in the distance.

PLATE 108   NEW HARBOUR AT ALEXANDRIA

The entrance to the New Harbour was defended by two forts on the promontories forming the tips of its huge semi-circular bay. The Fort of Qaitbey or Castle of Pharos, shown here, commanded the western promontory (see pl. 107) and the Fort of Pharillon or Fort Silsila the eastern. Nothing now remains of Pharillon, described by E.M. Forster as 'the obscure successor of Pharos, which clung for a time to the low rock of Silsila and then slid unobserved into the Mediterranean'. At the time of the French expedition, this fort consisted of the ruins of a square tower built on the tip of a line of reefs whose connecting dyke to the mainland had almost collapsed. During the Arab period, non-Moslem ships were forbidden to enter the Old or Western harbour (known as the Eunostos, meaning 'safe return', in antiquity), and had to use the shallower New Harbour whose exposure to north-east winds made entry hazardous in bad weather. The smaller vessels of the French armada anchored in the Old Harbour after the capture of Alexandria, but the large men-of-war could not negotiate the narrow passages between the reefs at its entrance. Admiral Brueys therefore sailed east to the easier anchorage of Abukir Bay, only to have his entire fleet sunk by Nelson at the Battle of the Nile (a few miles from the Rosetta mouth of the Nile) on 1 August 1798.

The new town of Alexandria that grew up in the Ottoman period on the neck of land between Pharos island and the mainland lacked distinction. The French found it sad and monotonous. The narrow, unpaved streets had no form of drainage and were always either dusty or muddy. With the exception of the warehouses, the construction and disposition of buildings was poor. The French observed that the 25-30 principal mosques, private houses, quays and other buildings were full of remnants of antique granite, marble, porphyry and limestone columns. There were altogether 88 mosques, 200 silk workshops, many workshops for making local cloth, some for leather-work, and 30 soap-works, using oils imported from Crete and Syria. Amongst the population were Egyptians, Turks, Arabs, Moors, Greeks, Syrians, Jews and some Egyptian Christians. The life of the town was lacklustre, human concourse taking place only in the bazaars and merchants' quarters. Trade was limited to the export of Egyptian grain, rice and natron, Arabian coffee and some Indian goods, and the import of sheets, silks, glass and other objects from Marseilles, Livorgno, Venice and Constantinople. Present-day Alexandria bears no resemblance to its depressed 18th-century forebear, being Egypt's second city with a population of several million, whose numbers increase substantially during the summer, when Alexandria is a bustling seaside resort.

PLATE 110   BAZAAR AT ALEXANDRIA

This covered bazaar no longer exists, but was the centre of 18th-century Alexandria's meagre commercial activity and local life, and meeting place of individuals from many nations. Watermelons and grapes, shown in the illustration, were typical produce of the Delta and greatly appreciated by the French in Egypt. The Europeans present in the bazaar, including one French officer, look no more incongruous than tourists in the traditional quarters of Egypt's cities today. The organisation of the bazaar, each product or trade occupying its own narrow stall, has not changed. The French were particularly impressed by the number of barbers in the bazaar in Alexandria, who put their patient's head between their knees and seemed about to decapitate it rather than to shave it.

The absence of marble, paint, a fountain and other decorative features in this house bears out the generally low opinion of the modern city of Alexandria expressed by the author of the Alexandria chapters of the Description, although the scale of the house is not unimpressive. The layout and design of the room shown in scene 1 is unusual, with its brick-arched bays supporting an open upper gallery with echoing brick arches, some of them springing from antique columns. The 'mashrabiya' (lattice-work) grills in the windows and delicate marquetry cupboards in scene 2 suggest that some Alexandrian residents had the taste and means to employ skilled craftsmen. The low level windows enable a man to look outside while sitting comfortably smoking his tobacco, while windows near the roof contribute towards better ventilation and cooling of the room.

PLATE 112   PUBLIC BATH IN ALEXANDRIA

This 'hammam' (public bath) in Alexandria is a characteristic example of a type of building for which Egypt was renowned. Indeed the hammams of Egypt were considered to be the most beautiful, convenient and best arranged in the East. Their floors were marble, their walls and ceilings brilliant white, and cupolas fitted with different coloured glass filtered a soft and mysterious light into the interior. In the centre of the spacious, lofty room where bathers rested after the bath, a fountain would lend a refreshing coolness to the air. No detail of pleasure or comfort was neglected. At the time of the French expedition there were more than 100 hammams in Cairo (the number in Alexandria does not seem to have been recorded), used regularly by all sections of the population and by both sexes. After enduring hot steam and vigorous massage, and passing through a succession of rooms of different temperatures, bathers would recline on sofas covered with rich fabric and cushions, sipping sherbet or coffee, inhaling aromatic tobacco, gossiping and exchanging confidences. Water was stored in huge cisterns, to which it would be conveyed by waterwheel from a canal or in skins carried by camel. Although this bath is small and relatively austere compared to the grand hammams of Cairo, it is an imposing structure, lavish in its employment of antique columns (some of whose capitals were used as bases, as shown in the top right-hand scene), arches and domes. Very soon after the French occupied Alexandria, at least one public bath was closed so that the troops could bathe and do their laundry. Jomard remarked that during the period the French spent in Egypt, the baths were less frequently used, especially by women. Hammams are still in use today, though mainly among the poorer sections of society.

To the French army, weary, thirsty and hungry after marching across the inhospitable semi-desert from Alexandria, Rosetta was the first pleasant experience since landing in Egypt. All the inhabitants were on their doorsteps, all the shops were open, and the town itself was impressive. Formerly a small port for ships passing down the Bolbitine branch of the Nile, Rosetta increased in importance after the Canopic branch — whose course lay nearer Alexandria -- silted up. At the time of the French expedition Rosetta was one of the major towns of Egypt, the entrepot for merchandise to and from Cairo, Upper Egypt, the East and Europe by way of Alexandria. Rosetta's population during the Ottoman period was far larger than that of Alexandria; its solid, red-brick houses, their entrances flanked by antique columns and façades decorated with patterns formed by alternate layers of wood and masonry, were much more imposing. The town was surrounded by luxuriant gardens and by the dense fertility of the Delta. Entering the Nile through its shallow, sandbanked mouth, the French noticed how, at some distance from the coast the blue Mediterranean was stained bright green, turning yellowish near the Rosetta mouth. It was while the French were investigating some ruined fortifications north of Rosetta in 1799 that Bouchard discovered the Rosetta Stone (see pls. 72-74).

PLATE 114   FOUEH AND PIGEON HOUSES BY THE NILE

According to Jollois, who wrote this section of the Description*, Foueh (shown above) was Rosetta's predecessor as the port and entrepot of the Bolbitine branch of the Nile. It was replaced by Rosetta in about the 9th century A.D., when the northward extension of the Delta, caused by the volume of silt annually poured into the sea during the inundation, required the port to be moved nearer to the Nile mouth. Between Rosetta and Foueh the river makes a series of bends, and Foueh itself stands at a point where the Nile divides round a small island, which Jollois found exceptionally picturesque. In 1798 Foueh was little more than a market town, distinguished only by the variety and elegance of its mosques. The village shown below is one of many on the Nile's banks. Jollois observed that Egyptian villages were built almost entirely of mud, the houses seldom more than 12 feet high but often surmounted by conical dovecotes in which innumerable pigeons gathered. Pigeons remain an important source of protein for village dwellers and scenes like those illustrated here can still be found throughout the Nile valley.*

The French were intrigued by the scenery and life of the Nile valley. One division of the French army travelled up the Nile to
Cairo from Rosetta, joining forces with another at El-Rahmaniya, just south of Foueh (see pl. 114), having marched from
Alexandria across the semi-desert. To Jollois, the fertile landscape of the Delta, animated by herds of buffalo grazing,
wallowing in the river or drawing ploughs and tended by the conscientious 'fellah' in his picturesque robes, was a delight. The
French were objects of great curiosity to the villagers, who would run out to watch them. Jollois particularly admired the
statuesque grace of the village women and the dexterity with which the Egyptians swam in the Nile. He was amazed by the
way that children of both sexes ran naked even in the fiercest heat, in singular contrast to the zealous care with which mature
women swathed themselves from head to foot. The discordant, monotonous creak of waterwheels on the banks of the Nile
could be heard from afar, ceaselessly pouring water into the multitude of irrigation channels that cut through the fields.
Although modern electric pumps are often used today to raise water from the Nile, waterwheels such as this are still a
common sight in Egypt.

PLATE 116   MONASTERY OF WADI EL-NATRUN

D eir Anba Bishoi (the Monastery of Father Bishoi) bears the name of its 4th-century founder, one of the famous monks of Scetis (later known as the Wadi el-Natrun), a desert depression between Cairo and Alexandria. Egypt was the birthplace of Christian monasticism, and during the 4th and 5th centuries the monasteries of Scetis attracted pilgrims from all over Christendom. Social and political unrest encouraged hermits throughout Egypt to gather together for safety, and all the desert monasteries huddle behind semi-fortified enclosure walls which were probably first erected in the 5th century to give the monks some protection from the marauding beduin. Deir Anba Bishoi, like the other monasteries in the Wadi el-Natrun, was sacked many times before and after the Arab conquest, and few of its buildings can be dated with certainty before the 9th century. Monasticism in Egypt declined as a consequence of conversion to Islam and natural catastrophes such as plague and famine. In the 18th century most monasteries lay in ruins. A visitor found only four monks at Deir Anba Bishoi in 1712; by 1843, when Robert Curzon went to the Wadi el-Natrun, there were 13.

B irket Qarun or Lake Moeris occupies the lowest position in the Fayum depression, lying 135ft below sea level. Its waters are brackish, the outflow of the irrigation system of the oasis, and the north shore is entirely arid. The lake was very much larger in antiquity, as demonstrated by the paved processional way leading from the former lake shore to the ruined Ptolemaic city Soknopaiou Nesos (Dime), which is stranded about a mile from the northern rim of the present-day lake. The oasis is entirely fertile and has long been renowned for its agricultural produce, wild fowl and fish. Senhur is a village on the site of an ancient town not far from the south shore of Birket Qarun. Jomard heard about catacombs in the area but was unable to locate them. He gave his impression instead of the minaret and elegant arches of the mosque, with some local inhabitants at prayer.

PLATE 118   A NILE VILLAGE AND MINYA

South of Cairo the agricultural plain on the east bank of the Nile is often very narrow, hemmed in by the cliffs bordering the high plateau of the eastern desert. Cultivation is restricted to a meagre strip of irrigable land, picturesquely fringed by the hazy blur of the barren hills beyond. The scene above shows a typical village, surrounded by palm groves and built of mud brick of which the only distinguishing feature is the domed sheikh's tomb. The largest centres of population between Cairo and Luxor are nearly all on the west bank, where the plain is wider. Minya (below, and see pl. 119) was a typical Nile-bank town at the time of the French expedition, of less importance than Beni Suef to the north or Mallawi to the south, which it replaced as capital of Minya province in 1833.

The city of Minya is 148 miles south of Cairo, between the Ibrahimiya Canal and the Nile. During the 19th century Minya became a prosperous agricultural centre. It is now a thriving university town, with an attractive frontage to the Nile and a number of dignified and spacious houses that have seen better days. Jomard, who wrote about Minya for the Description, was uncertain whether the city had a history going back to pharaonic times. He noticed, however, many signs of great antiquity in the mosques. There were splendid columns of granite and porphyry, superbly worked, and probably dating to the Byzantine period just before the Arab conquest. He observed also that many of the Nile quays had ancient blocks built into them. Champollion considered Minya to be the site of Menat Khufu, the ancient city where the builder of the Great Pyramid was supposed to have been born. It is now the natural centre for visits to the antiquities of the district. These include the tombs of Beni Hasan (see pls. 54, 55), where some of the local governors bore the title 'mayor of Menat Khufu'.

PLATE 120

ASYUT

Asyut is the largest and most important city in Upper Egypt. On the west bank of the Nile, it is the point of departure for the Ibrahimiya Canal which waters the provinces of Asyut, Minia and Beni Suef and from which, in turn, the Bahr el-Yusuf takes off on its long meander north to the Fayum. The city is surrounded by a large fertile plain extending both sides of the Nile, and it was from Asyut that the major caravan routes left for the oases of the Libyan desert and the Sudan. Asyut has long been one of Egypt's principal Christian centres, and church towers jostle with minarets on the skyline. The Asyut barrage, built between 1898 and 1903 at the same time as that of Aswan, regulates the water supply to the Ibrahimiya Canal.

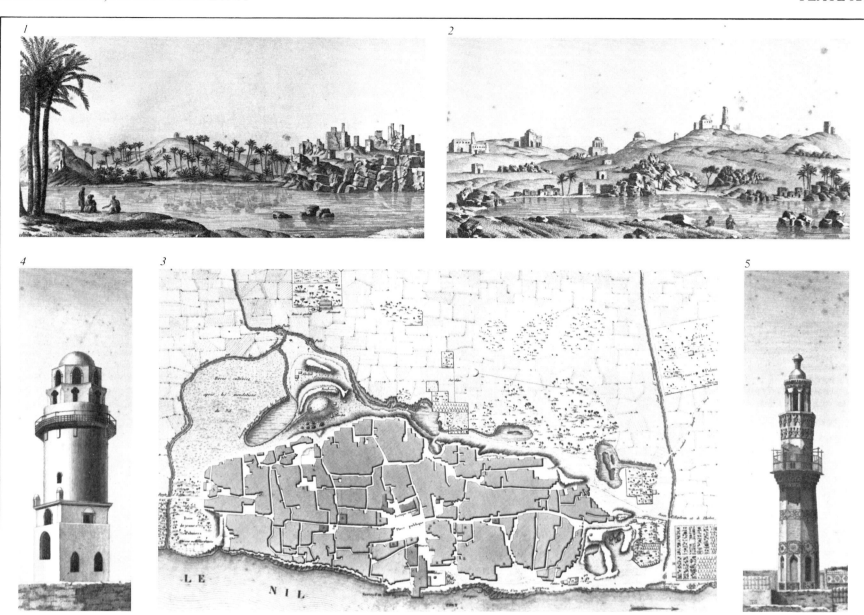

The French army reached Aswan, on the frontier between Egypt and Nubia, on 2 February 1799, eight months after Napoleon took Alexandria. It went no further. General Belliard observed the vast deserts to east and west, the daunting cataract to the south, and concluded that here nature barred his route. His division occupied Aswan for several weeks, enjoying its climate and amenities, while members of the Commission of Arts and Science sketched and studied the antiquities and landscape. No. 1 shows part of Elephantine island, site of the original settlement in the area, whose remains include a nilometer and temple. No. 2 looks across the Moslem cemetery which contains tombs of the 8th to 12th centuries; those with domes date from the Fatimid period. The building on the highest hill is a Fatimid 'mashhad' or tomb sanctuary, erected in honour of an unknown saint (sheikh). Just above the cataract the Ptolemaic temple of Philae stands on an island in the Nile (see pls. 1 - 2). The French invaded Philae, the southernmost limit of their occupation of Egypt, but remained there for only two days. Esna (nos. 3 - 5), 36 miles south of Luxor on the west bank of the Nile, is remarkable chiefly for the Graeco-Roman temple which is still half-buried in a depression in the centre of the town. In 1798 nothing but the 'portique antique' was visible, as marked to the rear of the 'place publique' on the plan. The minaret in scene 4 dates from the Fatimid period, the sole surviving portion of a mosque built in 1081 by the then governor of Upper Egypt. Like many other Upper Egyptian towns, Esna was an important centre of early Christianity. The minaret in scene 5, though shown on this plate, is actually in Asyut.

PLATE 122   CARAVAN ROUTE IN THE EASTERN DESERT

The French were astonished by the Arabian desert east of the Nile in Upper Egypt. Their southern campaign was vexed by the arrival of Arab troops from the Hejaz, who landed at the Red Sea port of Qossair and made their way to the Nile valley to support the Mamelukes. In order to thwart further incursions, General Belliard marched from Qena (north of Luxor) to Qossair in May 1799, crossing 150 miles of rugged terrain in three days. Until the 10th century Qossair was the most important Moslem port on the Red Sea. From Qossair caravans carried goods brought by ship from the Arabian gulf and India through the wadis of the Arabian desert mountains to the Nile valley, routes also used by pilgrims to Mecca. In antiquity porphyry, granite and other rocks were quarried in these mountains and dragged through the wadis to the Nile, whence they were transported to Lower Egypt and Rome. The French found the bizarre and picturesque appearance of the Arabian desert a challenge to describe. They marvelled at the infinite variety of forms, the numerous ravines and extraordinary ridges and veins running across the barren crags like ramparts taking off in different directions. They marvelled too at the veritable cocktail of colours -- white, pink, violet, yellow, green, grey, dense black -- and substances, amongst which they noted granite, breccia verde, porphyry, basalt, quartz, mica, feldspar, schist, gypsum, and limestone. At times the valley floor was wide and smooth, at others twisting and so narrow that only three camels could pass together, yet never did the surface present difficulty to the artillery. And this most arid desert was unexpectedly graced by acacias, growing in apparent defiance of nature.

T he French occupied Suez (Qulzum) without resistance on 7 December 1798. Napoleon went there himself shortly afterwards and received a delegation of merchants from the Hejaz, Muscat and Yemen. The town of Suez was undeveloped in the 18th century, but its strategic importance was substantial. The remains of the Ptolemaic fortress of Khysma to the north, and the Ottoman Agerud fort, built by Selim I, once commanded the land route to Cairo from the Red Sea. The French noted that trade, organised almost exclusively by the Greeks, was principally with Jedda and consisted of imports of coffee and exports of iron ore, tin, lead, grain, rice, cotton, linen, saffron, and other Egyptian products. Napoleon charged one of his engineers with the task of surveying the Isthmus of Suez to investigate the feasibility of cutting a canal to link the Red Sea with the Mediterranean. The engineer reported, mistakenly, that the level of the Red Sea was 29½ft higher than that of the Mediterranean, and the idea was not revived until, 30 years later, another Frenchman, Ferdinand de Lesseps, proved that the levels were identical. His scheme for a canal through the Bitter Lakes was supported by the Khedive Ismail. Work began in 1859, and the Suez Canal was opened in 1869.

PLATE 124   ST. CATHERINE'S MONASTERY

St. Catherine's monastery, at the foot of Mount Sinai, has preserved its integrity since its foundation in the era of Justinian (A.D. 527 - 565). Remote from any centre of civilisation, in the heart of the mountainous wilderness of Sinai, the monastery has withstood the vicissitudes of history and almost alone in Egypt maintains the traditions of Greek orthodox monasticism which prevailed at the time of the Council of Chalcedon (A.D. 451), when the patriarch of Alexandria was excommunicated and the vast majority of Egyptian monasteries broke away from the Christian mainstream to remain loyal to the Coptic Orthodox church. St. Catherine's history as a Christian site began in the earliest centuries A.D., when hermits clustered around the holy places of Sinai. In A.D. 330 the empress Helena, mother of Constantine, erected a small church and a tower to serve as shelter for the hermits at the site of the burning bush, around which the later monastic buildings were erected. The monastery has altered little behind its granite fortress walls since the 6th century, though the relatively greater security of our era has enabled the monks to demolish the protective precinct around the entrance door, and the windlass is no longer the principal means of access. On 7 November 1798 Napoleon received at his headquarters in Cairo a delegation of beduin from El-Tor in southern Sinai, accompanied by a monk of St. Catherine's; the beduin sought and received assurances for the safety of their caravans to Cairo, and the monk took back a proclamation granting virtually sovereign privileges to the monastery.

THE

MODERN

EGYPTIANS

Travellers had published accounts of journeys in the East throughout the 18th century, but the savants commissioned by Napoleon were the first to enquire in a detailed and systematic way about the arts, crafts, manufactures, costumes and customs of the modern Egyptians. Instead of the confused medley of travellers' tales, fact, fiction, hearsay and misunderstanding, the savants aimed to produce a firsthand, illustrated account and analysis of everything they found. They made comparisions with what they knew in Europe, and in a sense, the *Description* is a sociological treatise as well as an official report.

The compilers wished to learn from the Egyptians, and admired their achievements. The savants were, after all, connoisseurs of human skill and found much to praise as well as some things to mourn when they set about their task of recording in words and pictures what was left of the glories of one of the centres of the Islamic world. They enjoyed their task, but they found there had been many changes since the days of the Mameluke Baybars. In some ways the French had come too late. They were trying to describe the state of a nation exhausted by tyranny, and bruised by competition from the emergent empires of the sea-trading peoples.

The Egyptians in 1800 carried on most of the crafts that had made their ancestors famous, but the Ottoman Empire in its decline had affected the social structure and the economy to such an extent that wealthy patronage had largely ceased.

The Mamelukes had infused a new energy into the arts and crafts when they seized power in the mid-13th century, giving a new impetus to long established traditional skills, but they were conquered in turn by the Ottoman Turks in the 16th century. The latter at first encouraged the arts, but the empire fell into decline as the administration became corrupt. At the end of the 18th century the proverbial riches of Egypt had vanished like fairy gold as the tax gatherers extorted their tribute and did not allow the means to generate new wealth. Many workshops no longer produced their best, because the demand for expensive goods had shrunk. Mameluke palaces that had survived looting and destruction in the continual power struggles were in decay. Large four- or five-storey structures characteristic of earlier Mameluke times were no longer built. Thus architecture and the attendant arts of furnishing and decoration responsible for the myriad things that make up the contents of a house, suffered from the reduced economic circumstances.

Egypt was virtually independent of the Turkish Sultan by 1800, but this freedom was not used wisely by the latter-day Mamelukes, whose internecine strife and overbearing ways had alienated them from the mass of the people. To destroy the tyranny of the Mamelukes was the excuse Napoleon gave for invading Egypt. His savants were curious to find out the truth behind the legends and to see how much of the riches and skills of medieval Egypt survived.

Some major art forms had greatly declined. The production of high quality glass, perhaps reaching its peak in the intricately decorated lamps that became a chief glory in many mosques, had ceased. At the beginning of the 19th century the Egyptians did not even make their own glass, but imported the cullet from Venice, their ancient rival, and produced only plain bottles and glass vessels (pl. 147) for the sublimation of sal ammoniac from the soot of camel dung (pl. 148).

Some skilled trades continued: wood turners still made magnificent 'mashrabiya' screens, composed of thousands of expertly turned bobbins of wood carefully fitted together (pl. 169); but demand had fallen, as large houses were more rarely built or properly maintained. The turners had only basic equipment, relying almost entirely on practised skill, using hand, eye and foot co-ordination to produce the work (pl. 137).

The authors of the *Description* did their best to explain the methods used in Egypt to make essential goods. When a savant walked down the street and through Bab Zuwaila in 1800, he could see pre-industrial processes performed in open-fronted booths before his eyes, as was still the case to a large extent in France, and even England. The savants tried to describe accurately what they saw, as completely as they could. They were working in the tradition of the *Encyclopédie*, published 50 years earlier, which set a new standard for accurate and detailed description. The men of the Commission were confined within the conventions of the time, and their method of illustration may seem naive in certain cases. The artists of the *Description* were accomplished draughtsmen, and their work was subsequently reproduced by a team of printmakers. Etching and engraving was a time-consuming process, with a vocabulary of conventions, of cross-hatching and shading, imposed by its specialised technique. These devices of interpretation from one medium to another are now unfamiliar to those used to the continuous tones of photographs or photomechanical printmaking.

Because the artists assumed that European versions of Egyptian processes would be familiar, they did not always illustrate essential details; they believed that every schoolboy knew them. Few people in modern Britain or France will have seen the ingenious bow and string arrangement used for boring pipe-stems (pl. 153); but manually powered wood-turning lathes were the norm in 1800, and chair bodgers were a common sight in Europe. Northern Europe is now unfamiliar with the tinning of copper goods (pl. 145), although it is still practised in present-day Egypt. It was a common sight in Europe in the 18th century, since tinmen's shops and tinkers were ubiquitous. Thus the actual process is not illustrated here in detail. On the other hand, activities which seem self-explanatory are given what appears disproportionate space, as in the case of knife-grinders and barbers (pls. 149, 150).

The people of Egypt are shown in a sympathetic light without hint of caricature. Many of the illustrations are portraits, not 'types', and there is none of the vague and picturesque generalisation characteristic of earlier pictures and texts. The sturdy mariner, the skilled barber, the pattern-drawer with his apprentices embroidering are recognisable as individuals, going about their trades (pls. 161, 150, 140). There is a sensitive and sympathetic portrait of Murad Bey (pl. 157), once the enemy and then the friend of the French forces.

In the late 18th century it was still possible for intellectuals to believe that the sum of human knowledge could be encompassed by one person or in one publication. With the 19th century it became obvious that specialisation was the only way to sort the increasing flood of facts and cope with them. The *Description* hovers on the border between these two approaches, between art and science, with the advantages and disadvantages of both disciplines.

The French expected that Egypt would take on modern ways, and this was a motive for recording what they found before it was replaced by European 'improvements'. They did not foresee that once the exotic medieval structure was swept away, what took its place would have disadvantages as well. Many fine things typical of Egypt disappeared along with the bad, among them skills, architectural treasures, and ancient customs. Poverty, injustice, heavy taxation and militarism persisted; so that under Mohamed Ali, successor to the French and introducer of European ways, ordinary Egyptians were possibly worse off than before.

In small matters, as in great, these changes can be illustrated from the *Description*. The scene of the embroidery workshop in Cairo typifies the rest (pl. 140). As far as is known, such a workshop had always been headed by a master who drew the patterns, traditional but with infinite variations on that tradition, subject to evolution, but not to the tyranny of fashion. His apprentices carried out the work under his direction, and while there was a steady demand for high quality, the trade and its marvellous skills persisted.

In Europe at exactly the same moment embroidery was facing acute decline. The nadir was reached when Berlin woolwork, or embroidery by numbers, came into fashion. This could provide cheap, colourful, patterned textiles in the latest style. Printed cloth from Manchester could be imported into a country such as Egypt at a fraction of the cost of more elaborately decorated materials; the fashion for European goods took root and then the death-knell of traditional goods was sounded. Workshops closed as factories thrived. The illustrations of the *Description* are a salutory reminder of how fragile the structure of society is, and how quickly skills can be lost when demand changes.

CHARLES NEWTON

This type of machine, a 'sakia', was used in the Delta, and was powered by a blindfolded ox or water-buffalo. The device illustrated was drawn at the island of Farsheh, opposite Rosetta. It was able to lift water to a maximum height of 8½ feet, and was constructed over a large reservoir which was replenished with water when the Nile rose each year. Power was transmitted through a rather crude but effective system of cogs. The waterwheel itself was ingeniously constructed and built of better timber than the rest of the machine. The rim of the wheel was hollow, consisting of 30 or so chambers. Holes were pierced through the outer cover of the rim, through which the water entered and filled each chamber when it was at the bottom of its cycle, immersed in the reservoir. As each chamber rose, the water fell away from the openings and poured out through another vent pierced in the side of the wheel, draining into a sluice at ground level which fed irrigation channels.

PLATE 126   DOLAB

D olabs were used in gardens all along the banks of the Nile, from the mouth of the river to the First Cataract.
The water was taken from a sump in the form of a large well, deep enough to give a continuous supply of
water throughout the year. The well was replenished steadily by the waters of the Nile which filtered
through the subsoil. In this particular garden, the well was so large that two machines were used to draw water
from it. For more details of the construction of the machinery see pl. 127.

This kind of irrigation machine, a 'dolab', was common in Egypt. Like other kinds it was powered by an ox or a buffalo through a system of cog wheels, but it differed in that the essential means of raising the water consisted of an endless chain or carousel of water-pots. These were attached to a rope which ran over a large pulley-wheel at the top and descended to a reservoir at the bottom. As this wheel turned, it pulled up the full jars fixed to the rope. As each vessel slowly reached the top of each cycle, it tipped into a horizontal position, discharging its contents into a trough placed immediately below to catch the water. The trough then drained to the side into a small reservoir which fed irrigation channels. No. 1 shows a general plan of the layout of the machine viewed from above. No. 2 is a section showing the water-pots passing over the wheel at the top. No. 3 is a view of the cog-wheel arrangement. No. 4 is a section of the wheel. No. 5 is a vertical cog-wheel. Plate 126 shows the dolab in operation.

PLATE 128   SHADUFS

Shadufs were set up along the banks of the Nile to lift water into irrigation channels as soon as the level of the river started to decrease. As the Nile subsided, so the number of shaduf platforms had to be increased. At the back of each platform was a small reservoir from which the water was lifted to the next level until it reached the irrigation ditches at the top. The simple machinery was supported on pillars of clay and consisted of a transverse beam from which hung the bucket arrangement. The buckets, made of palm leaves covered in black leather, were attached by a rope to a long piece of wood pivoting on the beam and counterweighted with circular weights of sun-dried clay. The labourers worked in time with each other, chanting or singing to keep the stroke. They pulled down the empty buckets, plunged them into the Nile and let the gravity of the counterweight lift the water the six feet or so onto the next platform, where it ran in channels to the reservoir at the back.

The Arabs invented the means to produce loaf-sugar from sugar cane and it became an essential part of Arab cuisine. The process involved crushing the stems of the plant and gathering the juice. This was then boiled and the sugar crystallised by evaporation. White sugar was obtained by repeatedly boiling, washing and evaporating until the product was refined by progressive removal of any sediment. A blindfolded ox is shown turning the mill, which consisted of two rollers close set for crushing the cane stems and extracting the juice, power being transferred by a primitive but effective set of large cog wheels. A man is feeding the stems into the slow-turning machine. Another takes away a bowl of extract from the large receptacle beneath the rollers to pour through a sluice in the wall. This leads to vats for settling. Eventually the boiler was filled and after repeated boiling and settling the refined syrup was poured into cone-shaped moulds ranged along the walls. The sugar settled and crystallised into the shining loaves which were once a familiar sight in grocers' shops throughout the world.

PLATE 130   THRESHING

Threshing of grain was accomplished by means of a heavy wooden vehicle pulled by oxen. Within the wooden frame were three sets of iron wheels on wooden axles which, with a crushing action, separated the grain from the chaff. On an area of prepared ground the sheaves of the grain crop were spread out and the weighty vehicle was driven in all directions until the threshing was completed. Another man armed with a fork made sure that all the sheaves went under the cart. The grain was winnowed by throwing the chopped straw and grain into the air with forks. The wind carried away the straw and the grain fell to the earth.

The Egyptian plough, 'meherrat', was very simply constructed. It consisted of two pieces of wood, hinged at one end in such a way that the angle between them could be adjusted. This was done by means of a peg, pierced with a series of holes, which was fixed to the lower piece and slid through a slot in the upper piece, the beam, and was secured with a dowel. The lower piece was fitted with an iron ploughshare. This varied in form, according to region, from narrow and sharp, as illustrated here, to a broad spade-like shape. Rising from the lower piece of wood were two wooden handles, fixed with mortice and tenon joints, which enabled the ploughman to control the plough and push the ploughshare down into the soil.

PLATE 132

V inegar was made in Egypt from grape juice or from dates. The factories in Cairo were called 'ma'mal el khall'. The grapes, imported from Cyprus or the Greek islands, were crushed under a kind of millstone. This was usually cut from the drum of an antique stone column, shaped roughly into a truncated cone and mounted on to an axle fitted into a vertical post which also turned. The juice and pulp was diluted with water placed in vats and left to ferment for 15 days or so, depending on the temperature. This mixture was then filtered, honey added and further fermented into vinegar. Cheaper vinegar was made from dates which had been steeped in water and then squeezed under a large screw press. The juice was filtered, honey added and the mixture fermented out.

PLATE 133

DISTILLING

The principal product of a distillery in Cairo was a kind of brandy, called 'arak'. Date pulp and water was fermented, aniseed added for flavour, and the resultant mixture was heated and distilled in earthenware 'alembics' or stills. The alembics in the illustration were fitted with simple tubes which conducted the vaporised alcohol down into the water-cooled jars where it condensed. There were 10 or 12 such distilleries in Cairo at the time of the French expedition, and they provided a thoroughly unsavoury smell.

PLATE 134

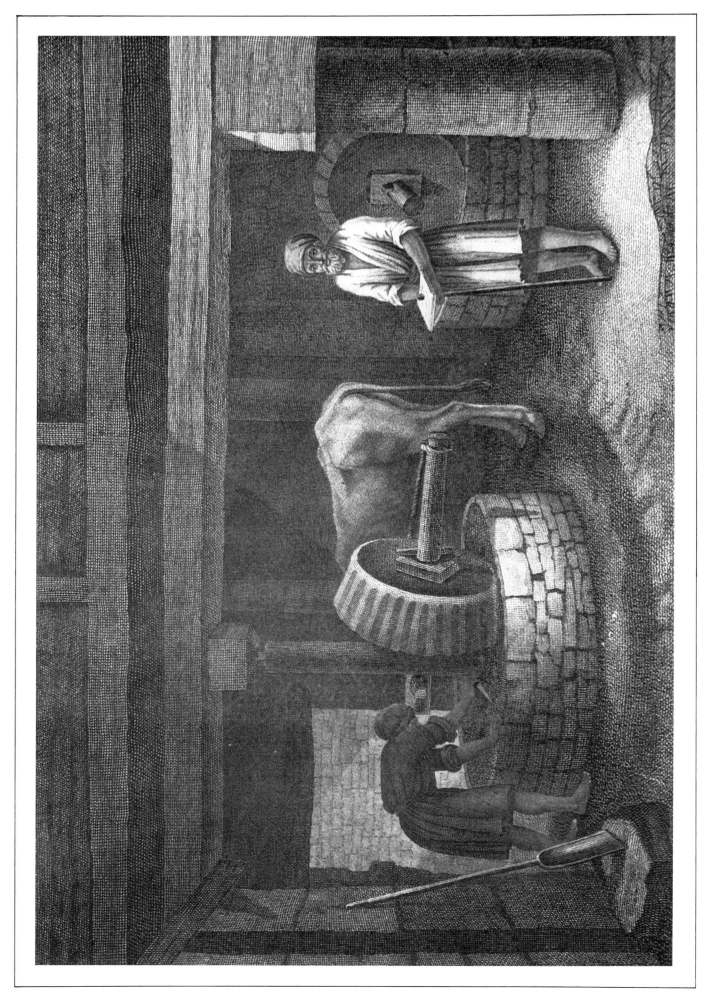

This plate shows the interior of a linseed oil mill. An ox pulled round a large millstone in the form of a truncated cone which crushed, and because of its shape, ground the seed, expressing the oil it contained. The workmen turned over the pulp with a wooden rake so that the milling was as complete as possible. They then placed more seed under the millstone with the aid of a wooden shovel as the crushed grains decreased in volume. The truncated millstone gave a much stronger grinding action than would have been produced by a simple cylinder.

PLATE 135

The looms of the Egyptians consisted of four poles fixed in the ground, with all the other parts assembled round this crude framework. The equipment of the loom was otherwise similar to that used in Europe. The warp threads were suspended above the loom and weighted with a stone. As the weaver progressed with his work, he rolled the finished cloth on to the beam in front of him. When the weight at the far end of the warp threads was drawn up to the roller mounted high on the wall, it was replaced by a batten and cords weighted with the same stone, thus retaining the same tension. The apprentices are shown winding the warps in preparation for the looms. The weaving sheds were usually large buildings which enabled a great number of looms to be accommodated. The linen produced was usually very fine, about 18 inches in width, plain or striped. This was used for clothing of all kinds, including shirts, the baggy trousers worn by men and women, and veils worn by the poorer women. A finer sort of striped linen was used as a kind of mosquito netting by those unable to afford fine gauze. Cotton was woven on exactly the same kind of loom.

PLATE 136

S cene 1 shows a craftsman using a small loom to weave elaborate braids used for trimming garments, cushions and other textiles. The loom was horizontal and the shed of the warp threads was suspended from above by a pulley and was operated below by the weaver's foot under the loom. He passed his shuttle through the shed of the warp and beat the threads down with a small rod held in his left hand. As the work progressed, it was wound on the roller furthest away from him. The braids were made of silk, often with gold and silver thread. One speciality was the richly decorated red silk sash from which the sword was hung. In scene 2 a cord-maker is depicted kneeling in front of his frame, weaving or plaiting his cord with great dexterity, using his fingers only, and securing it at each stage with a wooden peg. The tension of the work was maintained by a weight at the end of a cord which passed over two small pulleys at the opposite end of the frame. The weaver of woollen cloth in scene 3 uses a crudely constructed loom of rough wood, held together with nails and string. Its product was the basic cloth used everywhere in Egypt. The belt-maker of scene 4 might be weaving his product from silk, cotton or wool. The Egyptian liked a belt of bright and many colours; it had to be long enough to go twice round the body and was used to hold papers, money or a man's pipe.

The preparation of cotton is shown in scene 1. Cotton fibres require separation and teasing out before they can be spun. In Egypt this was done by means of a special bow. This instrument was held above the pile of cotton while the craftsman struck the string with a small mallet. The vibrations caused the cotton to separate from the mass and cling to the bow-string, then fall back, uncompacted. A boy then carefully wound the fluffed-up fibres round a small roller.

The wool-spinner of scene 2 uses a simple weighted spindle. The spinner held the loose wool in the left hand and turned the spindle with the right. A hook on the top of the spindle twisted the length that was being made and the completed thread was wound on to the body.

The spun woollen thread was wound on to bobbins using the apparatus illustrated in scene 3. A kind of fly-wheel made of wood and string was turned by a handle. A loop of cord transferred this momentum to a small bobbin at the other end of the machine on which the wool was neatly wound.

A wood-turner is shown in scene 4. The work was held in a lathe between two points and revolved with a looped bow string. The tools were gripped with the right hand and the foot, and were supported by an iron rod. Skilled workmen produced delicate work such as the 'mashrabiya' screens for windows.

A locksmith is at work in scene 5. Egyptian door locks were usually made of wood. The locksmith repaired old locks and made new ones. He is shown in his workshop, surrounded by his tools, gripping a piece of wood between his feet and working on it with a plane.

PLATE 138

DYE WORKS

The low brick platform shown on the left encloses large earthenware vats in which the dyestuffs were placed to form the liquor of an indigo dye vat. One of the workmen is shown stirring the mixture. In front are earthenware vessels, made from Nile clay, which were used for mixing the raw indigo with water after it had been ground up. The dye was then placed in the vats built into the brick platform. Cloths which have been dyed can be seen hanging from a line above the workman. The blue colour of the indigo developed as the dyestuff oxidised, and a deeper shade was obtained by repeated dipping.

T he apparatus used by the Egyptians to make rope was very simple. Four bobbins wound with cord were attached to a frame, supported on two crudely cut stakes. The frame was held upright by a cord attached to another stake fixed in the ground. The bobbins were revolved at equal speeds by means of an endless cord which went round all of them. This required two men. Another workman held the four cords leading from the bobbins and spun the rope evenly by hand, without using the fluted spindle normally employed in Europe. The fibres used by the Egyptians were obtained from the material that surrounds the bottom of the branches on a palm tree.

Young apprentices are shown embroidering textiles stretched on tambours, under the supervision of their master who is busy drawing more floral patterns. These patterns were applied to cotton, linen, silk, muslin and leather. Objects made from these materials included cushions, sashes and handkerchiefs given as gifts when visiting. Precious metal threads were often used, the pattern being embroidered on the back as well as the front. Leather was embroidered with great skill, often using a very fine silver-gilt solid filament which gave lustre and durability. Sometimes part of the design was outlined with pieces of appliqué leather.

PLATE 141

T he master felt-maker and his apprentices are producing a felt in the workshop by ceaselessly trampling and rolling backwards and forwards the dampened, felted wool inside the cloth beneath their feet. The raw material for the felt was carefully washed wool from lambs, sheep or camels. The microscopic scales on the individual hairs interlock and felt when they are pressed together, thus forming a solid, thick textile without spinning or weaving. The main felt-making district was called El-Lebudia, near the Hammam el-Gedid, the great bath of Cairo. Felt was much used for caps and turban centres, for mats, and most of all for horse-felts placed under the saddle.

PLATE 142   MASONS AND ROOFERS

Masons used a mortar composed of lime and earth to cement their work, which was of brick and quarried stone. They usually placed a sleeper of fir wood between the courses of stone every two yards or so, in order to even up the masonry. In the opinion of Le Père, the architect who wrote the original commentary on this illustration, this practice effectively prevented the wall from binding together properly. He said that another bad habit was to use thin wooden sleepers placed on edge on both faces of the wall. The area in the middle was filled with rubble and small stones, which meant that the structure was rendered even weaker. The roofer (below) first fixed reeds on to the rafters, often covering these in turn with matting. On top of this he applied a layer of mortar. The matting was not strictly necessary because the mortar would, with care, stick to the reeds alone.

1

2

The Egyptian carpenter (right of scene 1) always worked seated. The tool he used most frequently was a kind of adze. Slanted joints fixed with nails were more commonly used than mortice joints. The sawyer (left of scene 1), who cut planks, erected a temporary scaffolding against a wall. Ropes slung over the top of the framework, attached to two heavy weights, supported a beam which in turn held up one end of the piece of wood to be sawn. A simple movable stand held up the other. In spite of the flimsy appearance of the apparatus, it enabled two men to saw planks accurately. The joiner (scene 2) did not stand at a workbench but worked sitting down or kneeling. A plane similar to European examples was most commonly employed, as well as a rabbetting-plane. The joiners, like the carpenters, used an adze, but it was made smaller for the finer work.

PLATE 144 MATMAKERS

A mat-maker is shown in this plate. Mats were in widespread use in Egypt and the example seen on the loom, although large in size, was typical. The thick warp cords of the mat were interwoven with rushes, 'cyperus', or reeds, by as many craftsmen as could sit side by side on the bench placed beneath the mat. A batten with the warp cords threaded through was used to beat down and firm the work as it progressed. Mats were sold in the district of Cairo called El-Hosaria, and many of them were made in the Fayum.

The scene above shows a coppersmith inside his workshop, either tinning a copper vessel he has just made or re-tinning an old one. The boys are degreasing and polishing cooking pots and their lids by standing on a piece of matting dusted with emery powder or sand and moving it with their feet over the surface of the copper. When it is sufficiently bright, the vessel is heated, flux is applied and a bar of tin is melted against the hot copper. The molten metal is wiped over to form an untarnishable surface. The coppersmiths made cooking utensils, lanterns, plates, coffee-grinders and all sorts of domestic equipment. The Egyptian forge (below) was similar to European examples; it consisted of a masonry structure, at one end of which was the anvil. At the other end was the hearth, without a hood, and a pair of bellows. The latter was cylindrical and made of a single hide nailed to disks. The valves were situated in the centre of the wood, preventing the air escaping and cinders being sucked back into the bellows. The smith manufactured hammers, pincers, pliers, anvils for all the metal-working trades, window catches and hinges.

PLATE 146

POTTERS

A vast range of pottery was made in Egypt and only a small sample is illustrated above. The kilns were situated as near as possible to the beds of clay which supplied them. The workshops, often in ruined buildings or mere sheds roofed with palm trunks and leaves, were divided into four. In the first area the clay was chopped up, picked over and soaked in water. It was then puddled and wedged. In the second the pots were thrown on the wheel, in the third they were left to dry and in the fourth they were put in the kiln. Of great importance was the production of water coolers known as 'qulla' or 'abareeq'. These vessels were made of unglazed earthenware through which some of the water permeated and evaporated on the outer surface, thus cooling the vessel and its contents. Because of the low cost of the raw materials and the ease of production, many domestic utensils, and vessels used in the various manufactories, were made of pottery; often copying the shapes of more expensive metal vessels, plates and dishes. Only in a few workshops in Cairo were glazed wares still made. These were expensive items like coffee cups, or tiles inferior in quality to those made in medieval times.

The art of glass-making, which had reached such heights of skill in Egypt, had declined dramatically by 1800. The Egyptians no longer made their own glass but imported cullet from Venice. From this ordinary raw material they managed to make the domed lights for the roofs of baths, bottles like European ones, vessels for the manufacture of sal ammoniac, glass mortars for the druggist, alembics for distillation, simple oil-lamps and burnishers for polishing leather, paper and card. At this period there were only four glass-houses in Cairo. The glass-house illustrated was a large room, containing the kiln in the centre. The fuel used was maize stalks or bundles of reeds, some of which can be seen at the right of the picture. A craftsman has just withdrawn his blowpipe from the kiln; he is about to form a bottle from a viscous mass of molten glass stuck to the end of the tube by blowing down it. At the top of the kiln can be seen small holes which lead into the upper chamber, where the bottles were reheated gently and annealed.

PLATE 148   MAKING SAL AMMONIAC

This plate shows the interior of a workshop for the production of the useful chemical substance sal ammoniac (ammonium chloride). This was said to have been first produced in ancient times near the shrine of Jupiter Ammon. The substance is obtained from soot taken from chimneys where camel dung has been burnt as fuel. The soot was heated again in a furnace in special vessels which collect the sublimated ammonium chloride. The furnace emitted a dense cloud of fumes as it was slowly heated. A workman is shown crouched by the mouth of the furnace adding the 'kers' (dried camel dung) from the heap in front of the stoke hole. Through the open door of the workshop can be seen more vessels, luted or sealed with clay, drying in the courtyard. The workshop is roofed with joists made of palm-wood covered with leaves from the palm tree. A note to the original caption explains that the vessels are shown protruding too far above the top of the furnace, and it has not been made clear that the lower part of the vessel, below where the sublimation takes place, was not sealed with clay.

The method of knife-grinding in Cairo differed little from that of other countries except that the grinder used his right foot rather than a hand to turn the grindstone. Sabres, knives, 'khanjer' (long Turkish daggers) were sharpened in this way. The sandstone for the grindstones was extracted from the Moqattam Hills of Cairo. Unfortunately these low hills have vertical bedding planes, so that when the stones were chiselled out from the top of the hill, they were composed of different layers which wore unevenly. The stonecutters apparently ignored the advice of the French savants who urged them to cut the stones from one bedding plane.

PLATE 150

BARBER

The barbers of Egypt were so skilled that they took less time to cut the hair and beard than did a European barber to shave the chin. In the illustration can be seen the barber's equipment, which includes a magnifying mirror for the customer's use when he was being shaved. After this a rich man could have his beard perfumed. The chief skill of the barber was to cut the hair and beard of each man in a way appropriate to his occupation, rank, age and appearance. The razors were sharpened on stones from the island of Cos. They were then stropped by the barber on a strip of leather hanging from his belt. The barbers acted as manicurists, cutting the nails with razors, and they also sold depilatories. Many of them performed minor surgery as well.

The scene above shows a maker of edge-tools. This workshop does not differ much from that of the blacksmith; the bellows and the forge were the same, but a smaller kind of anvil was used. The craftsman made sickles, scissors, axes, hatchets, garden tools and 'qaddum', adzes used for various trades. In the plaster-mill (below), an ox slowly turns a millstone, made from the section of the drum of an ancient column. This crushes the gypsum on a lower stone, also a reused piece of ancient granite masonry, complete with hieroglyphs. The workman places pieces of uncrushed stone back under the mill and fills sacks with the powder, ready to go to the kiln.

PLATE 152   PREPARING COFFEE AND TANNING

The preparation of coffee is shown above. Coffee was drunk by all classes in Egypt. The beans were imported from Jedda and Yanbo in Turkish ships, landed at Suez and brought overland to Cairo. There the beans were roasted on copper plates, over a fire of reed-stalks, being continuously stirred with a little broom made of palm leaves. The coffee was then pounded in large granite mortars, while a child stirred the beans in the very brief interval between strokes of the huge pestle. Tanning in Cairo (below) took place in a huge complex of workshops in the El-Husania district. Skins of buffaloes, bulls, cows, sheep and goats were prepared there, using the waters of a lake called Birket el-Saqqayn. Morocco leather was produced in the Madabegh near the Soukkaria. The illustration shows naked workmen soaking and dressing hides in one of the workshops of the Madabegh.

Tobacco pipe-stems (chubuk) were made from a variety of trees such as cherry, lilac, jasmine or hazel. They were priced according to length, sometimes reaching over six feet. There were also cheap cane pipe-stems known as 'bous dokhan'. Many craftsmen had their workshops in the quarter of Cairo near the Muristan called Chubukshiya. They used a small drilling frame gripped with the foot, fitted with a thick brass wire, and surmounted with a drill-bit, 'metqab'. With a flexible bow and string they inserted the bit into the pipe-stem and worked it backwards and forwards to the other end. Another craftsman finished it with a boring iron to neaten and enlarge the hole. Expensive pipes were decorated with silk and precious metal braids. Some, made in two parts, were connected with a screw thread. Egyptians used pounded not shredded tobacco, mixed with natron to keep it moist. The wooden mortars were similar to European ones, but the pestles were quite different. They were long and club-shaped, the heavy top end providing momentum to the down stroke, the narrow end being used to pound the weed in the mortar.

PLATE 154

Preparation of fuel is illustrated here. There was very little wood available for fuel in Egypt and cooking fires had to be maintained with the dried dung of domestic animals. Children, mainly young girls, gathered the dung from stables in small baskets and took it to the women, who moulded it into small round cakes which they set in the sun to dry. The fuel burnt with a small flame and gave out a good heat with little smoke, finally glowing like charcoal until reduced to ashes. The soot from this fuel, unlike any other kind, provided the raw material for the production of sal ammoniac (see pl. 148).

PLATE 155

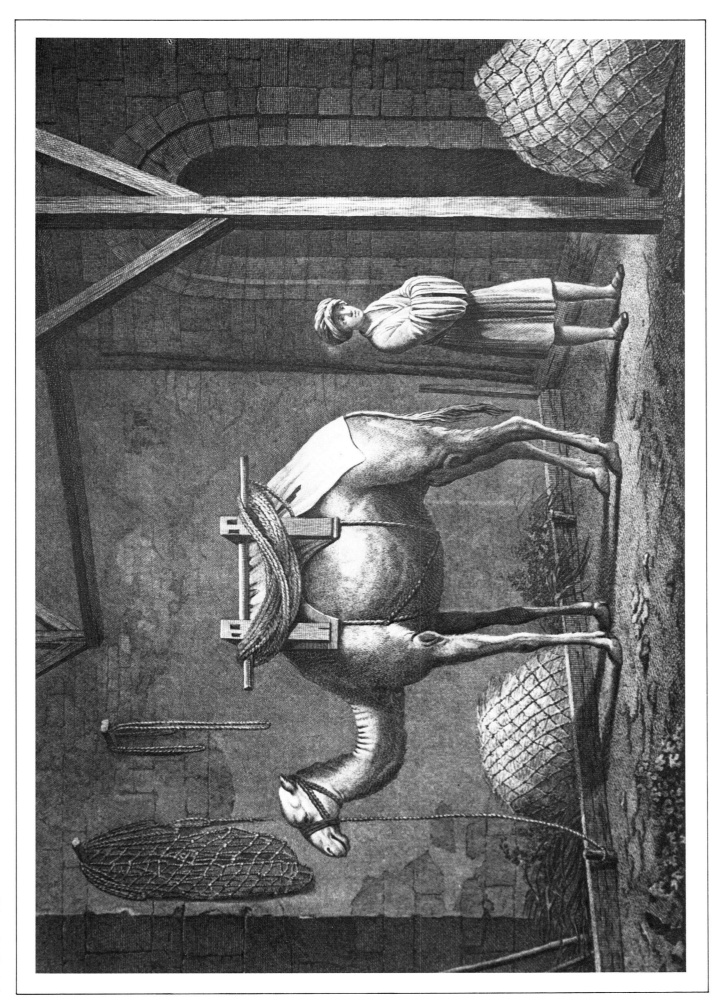

The camel driver of this scene emphasises the fact that goods in Egypt were usually transported on animals rather than wheeled vehicles. The camel driver provided the saddles and the equipment for the loading of goods. The camels were fed on straw, beans and clover, placed in a manger on the ground. In the towns they were watered every day, unless they were about to go across the desert; in which case they were watered every other day. The camel driver taught the camel to kneel and stay on the ground while the goods were being loaded. It was led by a simple halter round its head which did not impede the action of its jaws or muzzle. The pack-saddle had a wooden framework which rested on pads to protect the camel's back. The bales of goods were tied to wooden bars on top of the saddle.

PLATE 156   VEGETABLE GARDENING

E gypt was irrigated by using the floodwaters of the Nile, and one of the main concerns of the gardener was to distribute the water. Small square plots of land were prepared with the use of the hoe. The gardener moved the little earth dams to allow water to flow through the channels and blocked them again as necessary. The illustration shows vegetable gardens near Cairo, where the waters of a nearby lake formed by the rising of the Nile are being directed on to the little plots of cultivated land. The soil was easy to cultivate, a hoe alone being used to break up the clods, to kill the weeds and to form a tilth for sowing the seeds. The gardener worked with bare feet and planted, in the fertile mud, with the aid of his family, the seedlings he had already raised. The gardener supplied fruit, vegetables and pot-herbs in season to the dealers, as well as special herbs like a strongly scented form of the basil plant which was in great demand. Dates, oranges and lemons grew very readily, though the gardeners took little trouble with their cultivation.

Murad Bey was Napoleon's main adversary in Egypt. When Napoleon landed near Alexandria, he issued a proclamation that he had come to rid Egypt of the tyranny of the Mamelukes. Originally a Turkish slave caste, they had ruled Egypt at various times since 1250. In 1798 two Mameluke beys, Ibrahim and Murad, were in power, alternating the posts of 'Sheikh el-Beled' (Elder of the Town) and 'Emir el-Hajj' (Commander of the Pilgrimage) between them. Murad Bey and Ibrahim commanded the forces that opposed Napoleon, but they were defeated and Murad was wounded at the battle of the Pyramids. Murad was proud in bearing and appearance, formidable with piercing eye and long scar on the right cheek; he became wealthy by marriage, distributed liberally to his followers, and had a reputation for injustice, cruelty and arrogance. He built up an arsenal in Cairo and formed a flotilla on the Nile under the command of a Greek captain. In his house at Giza (pl. 104) he indulged his taste for music, chess and the society of literary men. This is the most acute of many portraits by the artist Dutertre.

PLATE 158   A POET

A poet is shown here awaiting inspiration, meditatively stroking his beard, seated on a low divan by the window in a typical Cairo house. His pipe and tobacco pouch are beside him, and the only indications of his trade are the books on the mat in front of him. By 1800 very little Islamic poetry had been translated into European languages and few people in Europe were aware of its combination of learning with passion and lyricism. Poets were respected, and every Islamic court deemed it necessary to have a poet on the staff to provide eulogies of the ruler and commemorations of great events.

An astronomer is shown here in an even grander interior than the poet's, by a window overlooking the roofs of the old city of Cairo. The ornate marble, wood and plasterwork decoration of the room is faithfully rendered. Near him is a celestial globe and on the table is his tray for reed pens and a combined inkwell and pen case. The Arabs had translated and improved ancient Greek treatises on scientific subjects. An astronomer was an essential part of virtually every eastern court; in early times the study of astrology and astronomy had not been separated, and indeed it happened that an astronomer might also be a poet, the example best known in Europe being Omar Khayyam.

PLATE 160

A MAMELUKE

A wealthy Mameluke is here shown against a sumptuous background. The Mamelukes ('possessed') were originally nomadic Kipchak Turks who lived on the northern coasts of the Black Sea. Captured or sold into slavery, they were brought to Egypt by traders. After a training not unlike that of the Janissaries, these hardy warriors were recruited into formidable regiments. They could rise through the ranks purely on merit, gaining immense riches and power, although still technically slaves. Eventually they overthrew the Ayyubid dynasty in A.D. 1250. The Ottoman Turks conquered Egypt in turn in 1517. The Mamelukes paid them annual taxes but soon wavered in their allegiance to the Turkish sultan. By the time of Napoleon they were virtually independent. Their customs and particular dialect of Turkish survived until they were massacred by Mohamed Ali in 1811.

The sailors of Alexandria, one of the most important ports of the Mediterranean, were noted for their seamanship. One is shown here in a coffee house within sight of the sea. He is seated on a bench, made from a fragment of an ancient Egyptian granite block, complete with hieroglyphs and covered with a mat. He wears an elaborate turban and smokes a chubuk. Behind him on the wall is the proclamation issued by Napoleon declaring that the French were pro-Moslem and had come to destroy the tyranny of the Mamelukes.

PLATE 162   GROOM AND PEASANT WOMAN

D omestic servants were very numerous, and an essential part of a rich bey's household was his 'sayis' or groom (left). He had to work much harder than most of the other servants, being obliged to run before or beside his master whenever he went riding, even if the weather was very hot. Sometimes he carried his master's 'chubuk' or long pipe as well. The sayis showed powers of endurance that amazed Europeans. In the countryside, the ordinary women of Egypt (right) were dressed very simply in a 'tawb', a kind of long shirt slit at the neck, made of blue cloth, a pair of 'shintiyan', trousers, and a 'tarhah', head veil. Being accustomed from a very young age to carrying heavy water-pots on their heads, they tended to walk in a graceful and dignified way. Their life was very hard with little leisure, as they continually fetched water, prepared food, spun cotton, linen or wool, looked after their children, gathered fuel, and performed many other domestic tasks.

T he Islamic world has no monastic tradition, but certain of its devotees have always embraced poverty in order to increase their religious standing. Some travelled great distances and lived by requesting alms which it was the duty of the devout to give. There were many kinds of 'dervishes', literally those who have renounced the world, and they were often credited with extraordinary powers, such as healing and magic. The scene shows two dervishes, from Abyssinia and Constantinople, seated in a coffee house, resting from their travels.

PLATE 164

EGYPTIAN PORTRAITS

Scene 1 is a portrait of the 'Emir el-Hajj', Commander of the Pilgrimage, who went with the great annual procession to Mecca. He escorted the 'mahmal', the lavishly ornamented camel-borne litter of state, and the 'khazne', or strong box, containing the money to defray the expenses incurred on pilgrimage. Ibrahim and Murad Bey, the adversaries of Napoleon, had both occupied this place of honour. No. 2 shows a Greek Orthodox priest from the convent on Mount Sinai, in striped robe and distinctive headgear, deep in conversation with an Arab from the Oasis of Firan. They are sitting on some ancient piece of ruined architecture, smoking their chubuks, near the sea-shore. No. 3 is a portrait of the 'Sheikh es-Sadat'. This was a title which indicated that, for his order of dervishes, he was the descendant and temporal representative of the Caliph Ali, first cousin and son-in-law of the Prophet. The sheikh was termed the occupant of the 'sejjadah', or prayer carpet of his great ancestor. No. 4 illustrates a very common sight in Egypt, a player of the 'rebaba', a kind of two-stringed violin. Accompanying himself with this instrument, the musician sang traditional songs of war and passion to an eager audience. No. 5 shows an inhabitant of Damascus, wearing a distinctive turban.

V*arious treatises on physiognomy had appeared in Europe towards the end of the 18th century (for example the work of Lavater). The plate may reflect this search for a classification of human facial types, as well as illustrating characteristic costumes and occupations. No. 1 is a boy from Alexandria. Males and females from this city were noted for their good looks, and this sensitive portrait in profile shows what was believed to be a mixture of Egyptian and Greek blood. No. 2 illustrates the grave features of an Abyssinian bishop. The ancient Abyssinian church preserved its distinctive rites, vestments and links with Coptic Egypt. Geographical isolation and the protection of the Moslem rulers ensured its survival. The woman of no. 3, with her veil lowered, is probably a Greek from Alexandria. No. 4 depicts an Ottoman dignitary, complete with large and elaborate turban. The word 'agha' had a variety of meanings, but this man was a very high-ranking official of the court. No. 5 shows the noble features of a 'sheikh' of Cairo. The 'dragomen', or interpreters (no. 6) often spoke five or six languages, and normally their services were indispensable for most Europeans. Murad Bey's dragoman was a person of great influence.*

PLATE 166

CAIRO PORTRAITS

The bustling streets of Cairo contained many kinds of traders with their goods. Their female customers went shopping wearing an all-enveloping cloak, a 'habarah' (no. 1), and veil to avoid the gaze of strangers. At home they would discard this cloak revealing a bodice (entari), trousers and jewels (no. 3). In no. 2 is a boy selling traditional brooms with very short handles, whisks and concertina-like waxed cloth lanterns. No. 4 is a donkey-boy, with beast ready-saddled to hire out to those who could afford to ride around the city. No. 5 shows a 'saqqa' or water-carrier; a goatskin filled with water is slung over his shoulder. The saqqas were in great demand through the hot season. No. 6 illustrates a sherbet- (fruit juice and cold water) seller with a large earthenware spouted pitcher on his back and a cup in his hand.

The variety of dress in Egypt was a source of amazement to European travellers. The exotic costumes of the Turkish soldiery had minute subdivisions according to rank, regiment and merit. The multiplicity of elaborate turbans (nos. 1, 2, 4, 11) or, in the case of the Janissaries, the sleeve-like headdress with a spoon container (kasiklik) in front (no. 3) simply bewildered foreigners. The Mamelukes had their own variants (nos. 7, 17), although they were superficially similar to the Ottomans in dress. The grander members of the ruling caste, the beys, had their own elaborate robes and turbans (nos. 5, 8), while the native dignitaries, the sheikhs (nos. 16, 18, 20, 21), had an even greater range of costume. Women, who took no part in public life, with the doubtful exception of the 'awalem' or dancing girls (nos. 13, 14), were even harder to illustrate for foreigners, since they were simply not allowed to see them at home, and much of the illustration must have been guesswork or copied from manuscript illustrations (nos. 25, 27). In the street veiled women were the norm and even brides were covered (no. 26). The Arab warriors were relatively soberly dressed (nos. 12, 15). Non-Moslems were subject to strict laws of dress. Jews were not allowed to ride on horseback (nos. 6, 22), and the robes of the Copts (no. 28, a Coptic scribe) and the Greek priests (no. 23) were distinctive. Court officials (no. 9, an usher, and nos. 29, 30) were also subject to elaborate divisions.

PLATE 168   WOMEN'S DRESS

'Awalem' or female singers and dancers often wore elaborate and expensive robes and trimmings. The full ensemble is illustrated in no. 1 where the musician is shown dressed in the complete outfit, holding a 'darabukkeh' or drum, accompanying herself while singing. No. 2 shows the simply cut but elegant red woven silk dress (a tawb) with broad sleeves. More skilfully woven and embroidered silk textiles used as costume are illustrated in nos. 6, 7, 8. In this picture the almah is modestly veiled (no. 4 shows the construction of this 'burgo' or veil). Around her waist is a woven silk sash with long fringes (no. 9), and falling from her head over her shoulders as a kind of covering or cloak is a 'harabah', usually made of black silk. The ordinary everyday dress worn by the poorer women is illustrated in no. 5. It was of the simplest construction and very voluminous, worn in conjunction with 'shintiyan', a kind of trousers, and slippers.

The Turks were originally nomads, accustomed to living in tents. The Mamelukes, originally from the northern Black Sea coast, had brought with them, as had the Ottomans, very elaborate tents which were their homes on military campaign and often the barracks within a fortress yard. Nos. 1 - 7 show the varieties of 'chadir' or tent. Some were very grand and used for the bey or pasha to give audience, while others were plain and meant for ordinary military use. Sometimes the tents were adorned with elaborately woven hangings, or composed of them. The windows on the upper floors of houses in Cairo were screened with a lattice composed of turned wood, a 'mashrabiya' (no. 8). These elaborate constructions were made on the simplest of lathes. Special ceremonies accompanied the birth of a child, who was put down to sleep in an ornate fret-work cradle (no. 9). In the heat of the day, a fly-whisk (no. 10) was an essential piece of domestic equipment. The floors of many grand houses were inlaid with a kind of mosaic 'opus sectile' (nos. 11, 12). Tiles were used in many houses and mosques: no. 13 shows a tile with a map of Mecca on it and no. 14 is a patterned fragment with a topographical view.

PLATE 170   ARMS AND ARMOUR

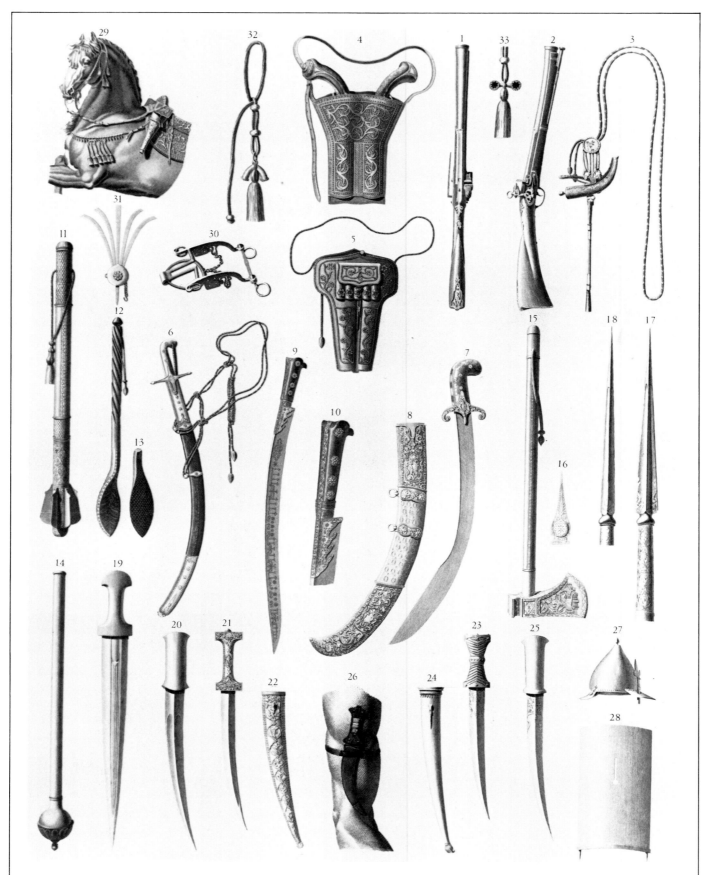

After the battle of the Pyramids, the French captured quantities of their adversaries' arms and armour. Nos. 1 and 2 illustrate the muzzle-loading flintlock blunderbuss with a short wide barrel that the horsemen carried. These guns were often ornately decorated, as were the powder horn and other accessories attached to a lanyard (no. 3). Pistols were carried, ready to hand, in worked leather cases (nos. 4, 5) attached to the saddle in front of the rider. Cavalry swords such as no. 6 were essential pieces of equipment, as were the carved scimitars with richly decorated scabbards (nos. 7, 8). The Mamelukes also made use of the 'yatagan' (nos. 9, 10), some examples of which were richly decorated on hilt and blade. Vicious-looking maces were in general use (nos. 11-14). Battle-axes had their place (no. 15), as did a selection of grim-looking spears (nos. 16, 17, 18). Daggers were made in a variety of forms, plain or lavishly decorated (nos. 19-25), one sort being carried ready for use in the heat of the battle, strapped to the arm (no. 26). The Mamelukes scorned elaborate armour, but used a Turkish helmet (no. 27) and a simple shield (no. 28). The trappings for a war-horse were adorned with tassels and decorative studs (nos. 29, 31, 32, 33), and the bit (no. 30) was skillfully made.

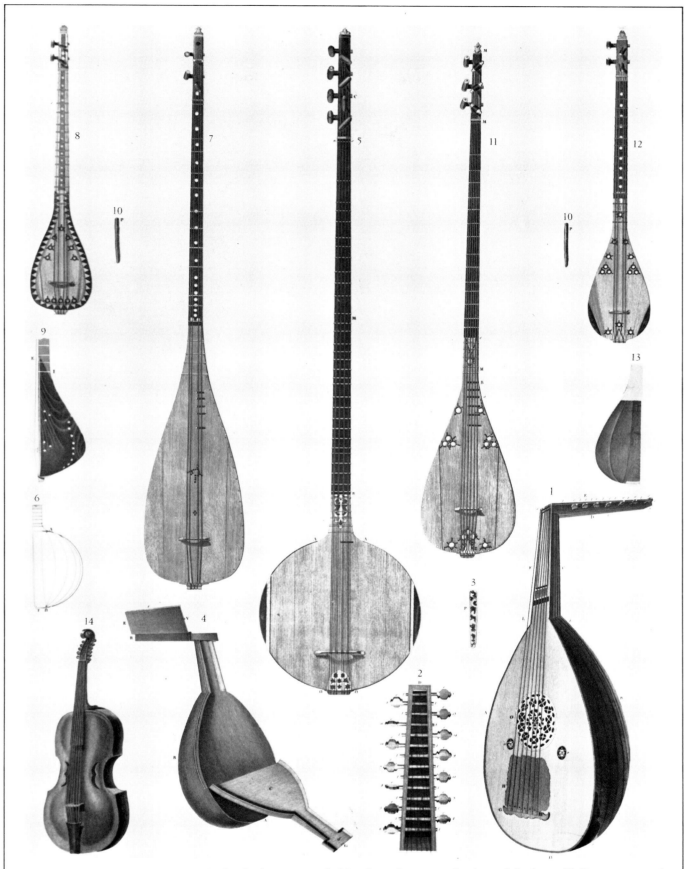

The Egyptians were passionately fond of music, and this plate shows a selection of the beautifully constructed stringed instruments in common use. No. 1 shows a perspective view of an 'ud', or lute, and no. 2 a detail of the tuning pegs on the neck. No. 3 is a plectrum for striking the strings. No. 4 is the leather and paper-covered case for this instrument with folding lids for the neck and body of the ud. No. 5 shows a 'tanbur kebir turki', which is a kind of large Turkish mandoline, about 4 feet 5 inches long. No. 6 is the profile of the body. Another kind of tanbur is shown as no. 7, the 'tanbur sharki', or eastern tanbur, perhaps originating in Persia. No. 8 illustrates a 'tanbur bulgari', or Bulgarian tanbur, which was lavishly decorated with mother of pearl and tortoise-shell; no. 9 shows the profile of its body. No. 10 depicts another plectrum and no. 11 is a 'tanbur bozurk', which is similar in form to the Turkish 'saz'. No. 12 is a 'tanbur baglamah', and no. 13 the profile of its body. No. 14 is a 'kemanjeh rumi', or Greek violin, similar to a European instrument.

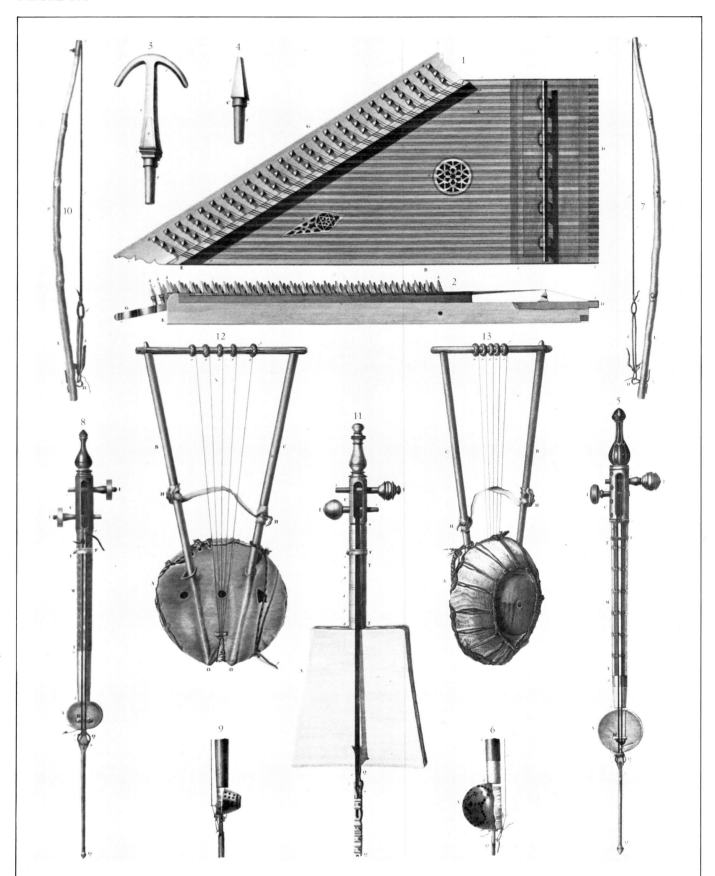

Among further stringed instruments, the 'kanun' (no. 1) was a kind of dulcimer, a hollow, flat instrument of great antiquity. The strings were arranged in sets of three. No. 2 shows the side elevation with a forest of tuning pegs, adjusted with a key which fitted over their pyramid-shaped tops (nos. 3, 4). The strings were struck with a plectrum made of a fragment of shell. No. 5 illustrates a curious kind of instrument, a 'kemanjeh a'gouz', played with a bow (no. 7) and belonging to the violin family. This was held vertically in front of the seated musician, its end resting on the ground. The body was a coconut shell covered with a skin (no. 6). Another instrument very similar in construction was the 'kemanjeh farkh' (nos. 8, 9). It was much less elaborately decorated than the previous example, being inlaid only with ivory in simple patterns. These kemanjehs were frequently used by the Egyptian equivalent of bards, the 'ashuk', to accompany their songs of love and battle. The 'rebab' (no. 11) was built according to the same principle but had a larger body. The 'kissar' (nos. 12, 13) was an Ethiopian instrument of a very ancient form and crude construction, being made of wood and sheepskin, with strings made of camel gut. It resembles the classical description of the kind of lyre that Homer used.

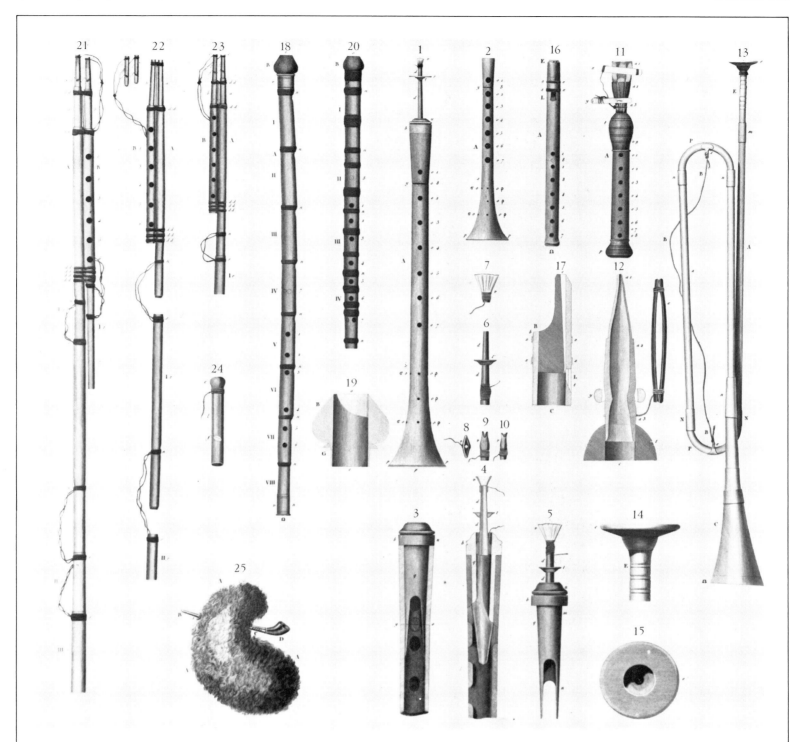

Among the many wind instruments the French saw in Egypt no. 1 illustrates the Egyptian 'zamr' or 'zurna', a kind of oboe made of boxwood, with a deep vibrating tone. Nos. 1-10 show details of its construction, including the mouthpiece and reed (nos. 6, 7). No. 11 illustrates the 'i'raqiyeh', a kind of flute with a reed (no. 12). The 'nefyr' (no. 13) was an Egyptian brass trumpet; nos. 14 and 15 show the mouthpiece. The 'suffarah' or 'shabbabeh' (nos. 16, 17) was a kind of recorder made of boxwood or ivory. The large 'nay' (no. 18) or 'nay shah' was a flute made of a single reed with a mouthpiece (no. 19). It was used in the ceremonies of the 'mevlavis', or whirling dervishes. A similar reed flute, the 'nay jiref' is illustrated in no. 20. The 'argul' or double flutes (nos. 21, 22, 23, 24), were constructed from reeds. 'Zuqqarah' (no. 25) were a kind of primitive bagpipes.

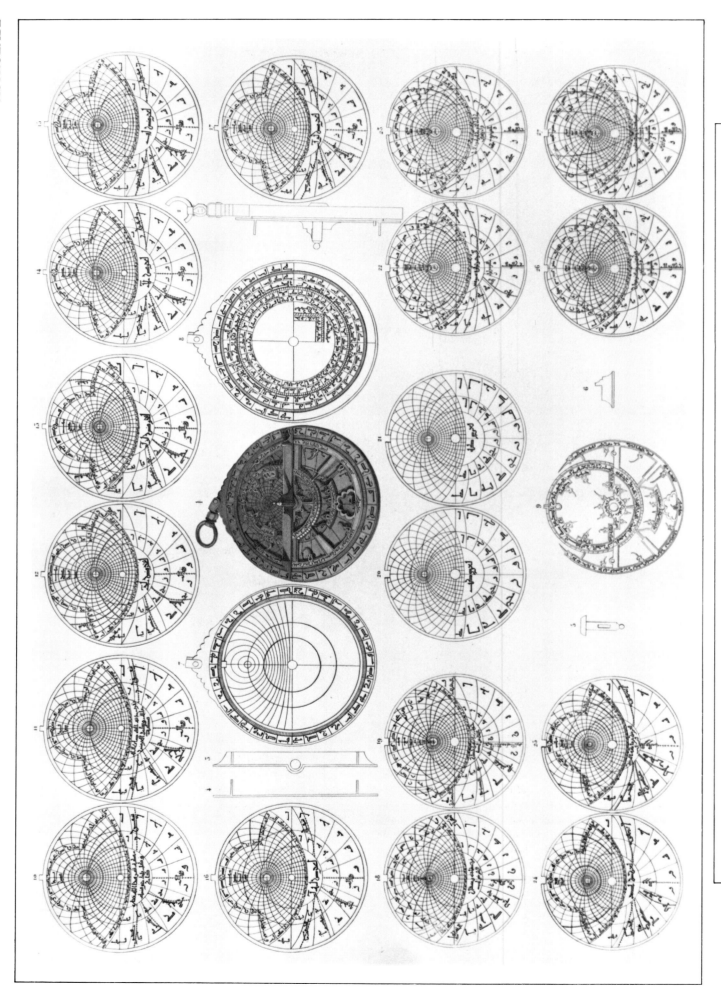

ASTROLABE

A planispheric astrolabe of brass (assembled in no. 1) is here shown with its constituent parts. The astrolabe is neither signed nor dated, but was probably made in Moslem Spain in the first half of the 13th century. It is engraved in a western form of Arabic script, 'maghribi' Kufic, using the Arabic alphabet to represent numerals; its diameter is 5½ inches. An astrolabe is an analogue computing device whereby astronomical problems are solved by simulating the apparent rotation of the stars around the celestial pole: a star map can be rotated over a plate, engraved for a particular latitude, showing the celestial pole at the centre, the horizon, the zenith, circles of altitude, azimuths, and unequal hours; star map and plate are in stereographic projection. Astrolabes were described by Ptolemy of Alexandria in the 2nd century A.D., and became popular in Islam, whence knowledge of the instrument was transmitted to Moslem Spain and thence to medieval Christian Europe. Astrolabes were used for teaching astronomy and for astrological practice; and in Islam, by the 'muwaqqit' of a mosque, who determined the astronomically defined times of Moslem prayer; sometimes also to find the direction of Mecca. This astrolabe belonged to the French orientalist, the Abbé Jean-Joseph Marcel (1776 - 1854), but its present location is unknown. Its design recalls the work of Mohammed b. Fattuh el-Khama'iri, an astrolabist who worked in Seville and of whom 14 astrolabes, dated from 1207/8 to 1223/4 are known.

LIST OF PLATES

195

CONCORDANCE

Description plate references are given in the right-hand columns. The volume numbers in the centre columns are listed under the two headings, 'Antiquités' and 'Etat Moderne'. An asterisk indicates that only part of the plate has been used.

	Antiquités							Etat Moderne	
1	I	3	59	V	3	117	I	8*
2		25	60		9	118		5
3		34	61		14*	119		4
4		37	62		13	120		3
5		40	63		10	121		1
6		46	64		8*	122	II	100*
7		47	65		11	123	I	12
8		49	66		18	124	II	103*
9		55	67		20*	125		III*
10		65	68		21	126		IV
11		67*	69		32	127		V
12		83	70		35*	128		VI*
13		88	71		34*	129		VII*
14		90	72		52	130		VIII*
15		91	73		53	131		VIII*
16		92	74		54	132		XI*
17		95		Etat Moderne		133		XI*
18	III	3	75	I	15	134		XII
19		43	76		23*	135		XIII
20		19	77		21*	136		XIV
21		20	78		29	137		XV
22		29*	79		31	138		XVI*
23		42	80		28	139		XVI*
24		40	81		46	140		XVII*
25		34*	82		67	141		XVII*
26			83		69	142		XVIII
27			84		70	143		XIX
28	II	20	85		32	144		XX*
29		26	86		38	145		XXI
30		33	87		33	146		XXII
31		31*	88		35	147		XXIII
32		3	89		36	148		XXIV
33		37	90		63	149		XXV*
34		91	91		65*	150		XXV*
35		51	92		20	151		XXVI*
36	IV	7	93		19	152		XXVI*
37		16*	94		41	153		XXVII
38		30	95		52	154		XXVIII*
39		12*	96		39	155		XXVIII*
40		25	97		50	156		XXIX
41		33*	98		55*	157		G
42		39	99		56*	158		B*
43		40	100		51*	159		B*
44		42	101		51*	160		D*
45		43	102		25	161		D*
46		45	103		45	162		A
47		46*	104		17	163		C*
48		51	105	II	84	164		E
49		54*	106		89*	165		F
50		55	107		87*	166		J
51		56*	108		85	167		K
52		57	109		95*	168		LL
53		59	110		96*	169		GG*
54		65	111		92	170		NN
55		66*	112		94*	171		AA
56		69	113	I	81	172		BB
57		72	114		79*	173		CC*
58	V	1	115		78*	174		HH
			116	II	105*			